BIG BILL BLUES

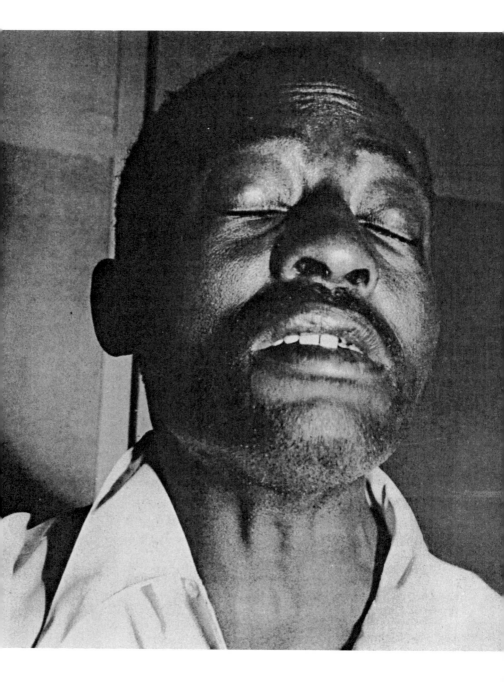

Big Bill Blues

WILLIAM BROONZY'S STORY

as told to

YANNICK BRUYNOGHE

*with 9 pages of half-tone illustrations
and four drawings by*

PAUL OLIVER

Foreword by Charles Edward Smith

OAK ARCHIVES

Oak Archives
An Imprint of The Music Sales Group
257 Park Avenue South
New York, NY 10010

New material in this edition:

Foreword by Charles Edward Smith

Introduction by Yannick Bruynoghe

**Revised discography by Albert J. McCarthy,
Ken Harrison and Ray Astbury**

**Additional biographical notes by
Yannick Bruynoghe**

Library of Congress Card Catalogue #64-8787

CONTENTS

FOREWORD

by STANLEY DANCE

This book opens a door on the world of the blues and their singers, a world that is very much a part of America, yet withdrawn and little known.

The blues that Big Bill Broonzy sings and talks about had an indisputably rural origin amongst the Negroes of the southern United States, but they were adopted by the coloured communities of the big towns so long ago that authenticity is not always precisely to be determined. Yet though rural and urban conceptions intermingled considerably and gave rise to great differences in lyrics, delivery, and accent, in the South the rural type is still predominant and relatively unadulterated. There, where men are closer to Nature and more dependent upon the soil, the old blues are not yet out of style. Nor are they likely to be 'so long as the South grows cotton and mules and men eat cornbread'. These are the blues Big Bill loves and seeks to perpetuate.

The way he has maintained his integrity as a folk artist is in itself a remarkable achievement. His blues took him from a Mississippi farmstead to the night clubs and recording studios of Chicago, to New York's Carnegie Hall, and to the cities of Europe, where the different circumstances and pressures might have brought about commercialization, or the vitiation of self-conscious artistry witnessed in others. Yet when he is heard singing, in person or on records, he is found true and unspoiled, the finest possible example of the authentic blues singer, and very much a man.

The material of his songs is rich in variety. Not all blues are songs of lament or protest. The tragic and the oppressive are faced and mocked with courage and humour. The droll

7

accounts of imperfect relationships between men and women contain more irony than self-pity. And when it is time to dance, Big Bill swings the blues on his guitar with a beat and an abandoned gaiety that leave no doubt as to how and why the blues are the backbone of jazz.

Yannick Bruynoghe, whose wonderful idea it was to gather Big Bill's stories and blues together, has been incredibly successful in setting them down in all their natural vigour and spontaneity. The astonishing anecdotes that Bill tells in illustration of his life and songs are the more vividly real for being in his own direct, uninhibited language. A book like this can only have been accomplished by the most faithful and understanding collaboration.

INTRODUCTION
To The American Edition

by Yannick Bruynoghe

It has been said that a bottle of whiskey and a tape recorder were the necessary tools for the making of this book. One bottle of whiskey is a fantastic understatement, but no tape recorder was ever used.

It was in 1953, after reading some of the usual literature about the blues, that Big Bill decided to write a book he wanted to be called *The Truth About The Blues*. He then started writing a series of short stories of all kinds which finally, after some rewriting and various modifications, composed this *Big Bill Blues*.

More than being the truth about the blues, it is the truth about a man whose psychology it perfectly reflects. This man having been one of the great blues representatives of this time, it is also *his* truth about that period and all that made his life and his blues.

The stories that he tells have many characteristics in common with the blues. Such a singer is, of course, a born story-teller, a sort of modern fabulist, with the faculty of easily "dressing up" facts in a way that makes them quite unbelievable but in depth so much more provocative. This also a very natural facility of adopting the personality of other individuals—how, otherwise, would the blues be as impressive if they were sung in the third person or as a story that happened to someone else?

So Big Bill may sometimes have adapted for his own use stories that happened to others, or that he had heard of, colouring them with his lively imagination. But it is nevertheless evident that he led a very hectic life, typical of most southern blues singers of this time.

9

On the other hand, there seems to have been not a little confusion in Big Bill's memory concerning dates and the birthplaces of some of his colleagues, though some of these mistakes contrast strangely with the accuracy of his memory about other facts.

Some suppositions may be put forward as a possible solution to this problem: after Big Bill's death on August 15, 1958, in Chicago, official papers had to be produced. His twin sister, Lannie, had proof that she was born in 1898 on June 26 — which would mean that Big Bill was five years younger than he pretended.

This changing of age was not uncommon amongst Southern Negroes of his time, for military, social, prestige or several other reasons, and it seems that Big Bill had a few. Hence some of his probable confusions concerning certain of his youthful activities or the exact situation of particular events.

So fas as possible, these errors have been corrected, mainly where other musicians are mentioned who have been questioned since the first edition of this book. The reader will find notes wherever these corrections could be made or where there is a precise reason to doubt Big Bill's assertions. He, is it necessary to say, wrote everything from memory and always with the greatest love for the blues.

We have not found it necessary to change details about recordings dates or titles. The discography at the end of this book has been revised as completely as possible. Titles mentioned by Big Bill may have been changed by the companies, or kept unissued, and, of course, so far as composer credits are concerned, we think nobody can pretend to know the exact origin or authorship of the numbers used by blues singers, especially in that time of collective tradition-making.

All this said, we think the key to this book, to Big Bill's intentions in writing it and in our helping him as best we could, is to be found in the. "envoi", the blues singer's own conclusion.

BIG BILL AND THE COUNTRY BLUES
(foreword to the American Edition)

by Charles Edward Smith

*"I'd go out in the woods and get up on a stump and sing.
Boys thought I was crazy. They'd say, 'Boy, you're the
craziest guy in Langdale!' "*— Big Bill.

"Everyone knows Big Bill." The speaker was Old Vic actor, John
Neville, the time, the 1950's. "Who doesn't?" he added somewhat
rhetorically.

Studs Terkel looked at this enthusiast fresh from London who
was, he saw, being quite serious. "Ninety-nine out of a hundred of
his countrymen have never heard of him," Studs told him flatly.

Neville looked his amazement. Big Bill Broonzy's concerts had
made something of a stir in England, as they had on the Con-
tinent. But *this* was Bill's home. And Studs knew whereof he
spoke. While the down-to-earth, country-born blues were still
largely confined to clubs of the South Side—Chicago's equivalent
of New York's Harlem— Studs put blues singers on the air, giving
Chicago and the mid-west first-rate documentary programs such as
that preserved in the history-making album, "Big Bill Broonzy
Interviewed By Studs Terkel" (Folkways FG 3586).

When fame came to Big Bill, there in Chicago in the 1950's, it
was a lopsided fame. In jazz clubs, to those who had ears for
country blues, he was incomparable— the others kept on drinking
and talking. Though rhythm and blues singers of genuine blues
calibre, such as Muddy Waters, respected him, the young and
knowing (and rock and rolling) called him "down home" and the
words were like shutters on the sound. There were others, many

11

of them the middle-aged or the aging—like Bill, from the deep South—who breathed a sigh when the term "down home" changed from one of derision to one of warmth and belonging, almost at the flip of a coin. Those who didn't see the glint of the coin— some of them would, later—walked out on Bill—and of course he'd known it, even without the chair-scraping.

At places like Silvio's, older people came regularly when Bill was there, to share the songs of home, the black belt blues. And like a slow trinkle, the new young blues fans. He also played occasionally, at concerts and clubs, before completely different audiences. When he appeared at the Blue Note, a jazz club, Count Basie, Benny Goodman, some of the younger jazzmen as well, gave him the musical recognition that, when all is said and done, means as much to a folk artist as to another. And there was something more difficult to define, that wove a link between the Blue Note and Silvio's. Duke Ellington, born and brought up far from the cotton fields and levee camps, who had an understanding of yesterday and tomorrow and people, sat in the dimness at the back of the room and listened. "Oh, that Bill," he was heard to whisper, "there's only one of him. I love him."

Big Bill was striking in appearance. Big, dark, broadshouldered, people turned as he walked by. When his face wore a bland look, as it did sometimes, you wondered what he was keeping the lid on. A burst of laughter and some of his foolish horseplay? A secret hurt and violence of thought? A scrap of song to catch the fancy of children? All these things and more would be possible. Bill was immersed in life, the raw, the rough, the commonplace. He could be withdrawn and brooding one minute, erupting in loud laughter the next—and neither mood the real one. Once, at a recording session—and apparently it often happened; he mentions it in his story—he seemed to have to break through a certain resistance before he began really to sing. Up to then it was entertaining but a shade casual. At a certain point voice and guitar deepened in intensity—and the way he stood, sat, leaned—arms, shoulders, facial features—all seemed part of the song.

"What is a blues singer, a good one or a bad one?" asks Big Bill (text). "I say he's just a meal ticket for the man or woman who wears dollar-signs for eyes." As for factual details antecedent to this and other home truths, you'll find some that are "out of true," so to speak, particularly in chronology. Perhaps you'll accept these as part of the real story, facts notwithstanding. (These flies in the buttermilk remind one of that sofa in Rousseau's jungle painting; the artist's claim was that he needed a spot of red just there.) Bill's mother may have been born in slavery but would still have been a bit young to mix love and cotton picking. On the other hand, who can doubt that when she lived in a shack outside Little Rock and Bill came to see her, he left the guitar outside, knowing her old fashioned prejudices about that sinful instrument? At his 1940 appearance in Little Rock—"First time I was booked in Arkansas . . . she just stood there at the door, she didn't come in, just stood there." and Bill added, because it seemed important to him, "When they found out who she was, they didn't charge her nothin'." And Crying Mary, who had to be beaten before she'd cook for the track-lining gang—however pathetic, she seems as real to us as the shout of John Estes:

> "Is every motherchild got a hold? If not, get one and a good one."

"Studs Terkel wasn't so far off in his estimate of Big Bill Broonzy. What he said was, "Bill spoke the truth, *his* truth. Always."

According to Hugues Panassie's "Guide To Jazz" (Houghton, Mifflin, 1956) Bill was born June 26, 1893, at Scott, Mississippi. He was one of seventeen children and learned to work early in life and late in the day. We are told that he was christened William Lee Conley Broonzy, that he had a half brother named Washboard Sam with whom he recorded some good and some bad blues, that he spent his formative years in Arkansas and travel between there and his native state. By 1915 he was share-cropping. When, the following year, drought ruined the harvest, Bill went into the coal mines. He was a Negro in the A.E.F. and came home, not quite the same country boy he had been. He was restless and resentful; it wouldn't be long before he'd be north in Chicago, working for the Pullman company and boning up on guitar from that veteran of the "race" record catalogs, Papa Charlie Jackson. Though it was rarely caught in early recordings, there appeared in Bill's singing a note of protest, not neat and tidy but tucked in among the good and bad blues.

Though he was a leading figure in commercial blues during the 1930's he was surprisingly little known outside this ground floor operation of "rhythm and blues" (as it became known to the industry). Some blues and jazz enthusiasts knew his records but their numbers were few, their influence slight. Until, that is, such influence was used to bring Bill Broonzy before a new public, and this happened, thanks to John Hammond, who brought him to

New York and Sterling Brown, who introduced him at Carnegie Hall.

"Unforgettable" was the word Irving Kolodin used to describe Big Bill's first concert appearance. The *rapport* the audience felt between jazzmen of the cities and a country blues singer had an extraordinary impact. As for Big Bill Broonzy, his stature as one of the great country blues singers took hold slowly, beginning around the time of that appearance at the 1939 "Spirituals To Swing" concert at Carnegie Hall, New York City. A mere matter of months and he made another debut, this time to a segregated audience in Little Rock. He made records when opportunity offered and, for the rest, made a living however he was able—molder, cook, piano mover, porter . . . "None of us would ever make enough money just playing music," Bill told Art Hodes (*The Jazz Record*, March, 1946). "I had to have my day job and play music at night." And ten years later (*Oakland*, Cal., *Tribune*, 1956) he summed it up: "I always worked at all kinds of hard jobs. I never was able to rely upon my own music alone till 1953."

How is it that one of the most popular artists on the "race" lists—then the trade term for the Negro market—found it so hard to make ends meet? Even a free spender should have had more to show for it than a second-hand Cadillac and a new guitar. In response to a query on this point Studs Terkel wrote, "No matter how relatively successful he was in the recordings of the Thirties, he had to find other work to survive. Fortunes must have been made euchering artists like Bill." Between the greed of promoters in his most "commercial" period—an experience shared by fellow blues singers—and the sharp decline of interest in the country blues among the younger generation, Bill's ego took a beating. By 1950, his ebullient optimism had simmered down considerably.

Meanwhile the early hootenannies—those informal entertainments that helped spark the folk revival—had awakened interest in folk and topical singing throughout the country and Bill made many new friends. After a summer visit to Iowa State College at Ames with an "I Come For To Sing" group out of Chicago, he stayed on as janitor. Some socially sensitive fans resented the mop-and-pail "gag" photograph of him in overalls, without knowing all the facts. Bill liked the place and said he wouldn't mind living there. A faculty member got him the job. Not that it was a job so much as it was a breathing spell. During this period he picked up new songs and dug into his own past for songs half-forgotten. He was often a guest at the home of the college president and sometimes visitors dropped in to whom Big Bill Broonzy was better known than members of the faculty.

The country blues drew upon a warp and woof of folk music, weaving a fabric that was sometimes a gaudy patchwork, sometimes a simple pattern, breath-taking in its sureness of design. The blues are not really very old by that name, possibly not much older than jazz, which *acquired its name* only in this century. Unlike some urban singers of the South, who have (though not all of them with equal conviction) recalled that the blues were known by that name long ago, rural singers have often insisted— as Big Bill did—that the name for them was not in common use until well into this century. But though the blues, by that name, may have been rare before the 1890's, the songs themselves may very well be as old as the spirituals. There has even been some intriguing speculation that the lyric form has West African antecedents. Blues had emerged from the welter of Negro folk music most forcefully by the 1890's, providing yet another Minority Opinion than that of Justice Harlan in *Plessy* v. *Ferguson,* the Supreme Court's endorsement of segregation. For it was the cry of a people as well as song or a way of singing it. Later on, when the blues were rising commercially, documentary recordings were almost non-existent, a factor which tended to obscure the complex relationship of blues to work songs, chants and hollers, as well as to other secular music.

Though sacred and "sinful" songs were often regarded as incompatible—and there were those who would sing the one but not the other—tonal and rhythmic heritage knew no such barrier and was in some respects the same for both. (This was demonstrable in the spirituals of Blind Willie Johnson.) The number of singers known to have sung both but who kept them in separate compartments, increases with our knowledge of singers and songs. Each, of course, had its own millieu. This was dramatized for him when Big Bill had to choose between being a part-time preacher or a country fiddler who sang songs. For those who love the blues, which preach in their own way, the choice was a happy one. And though Bill perfected his country style in cities, it became steadily stronger in its basic elements so that it was, as it seemed, even more genuinely an outgrowth of Negro folk music.

The country blues singer, while he remained in that environment, was not limited to blues. He played and sang all manner of songs and supplied music for dancers. Often he was involved in some phase of church music as well. He was country cousin to those itinerant singers/piano players whom Jelly Roll Morton

15

called "single-handed entertainers." When the blues singer struck out on his own he kept the tools of his trade with him and, at first—in medicine shows, minstrels, vaudeville—not only the styles but a wide variety of songs. As to the tools—you have only to look at early blues and jazz recordings, or, for that matter, the listings in Bill's discography, to find one or more of the many instruments used in folk music—jug and bones, fiddle and banjo, guitar and washboard, harmonica and washtub bass. Many a blues pianist, playing the "jookin' joints" (as they were called before there were juke boxes) had a touch of the banjo, guitar and fiddle in his playing. The mobility of musical influence is one of the least predictable elements in it. As a youngster—at a time when Ma Rainey climaxed her tent show performances with blues—Bill Broonzy was a country musician, fiddle and voice, supplying music for dancers and singing songs at "two-way" picnics—picnics that were segregated but shared the same music, from the same rude platform.

Though the term *blues* was late in taking hold—and given a tremendous boot on the popular music scene when W. C. Handy first published one—the word had been used in songs and about songs long before coming into general use. Many blues lines were common coin in the 19th century. The *slow drag* was a dance form adapted from blues and was used by ragtime composers; Scott Joplin included one in his folk operetta, *Treemonisha*. In New Orleans blues adaptations went all the way from slow drags to stomps. The "coon shout," which was called that even in the leading Negro weekly, *The Freeman,* was closely related to "shoutin'" blues style. And the blues went right on shouting even as the "coon shout" went into decline—big city blues men such as Joe Turner and Jimmy Rushing didn't have to go to vaudeville for inspiration!

In its urban development, despite the use of other bar-lengths (and countless musical hybrids), the 12-bar blues became accepted as the "classic" form. And indeed it is. But its basis is the four-bar line which, obviously, can be put into any number of combinations and has been. (Should you wonder why Bessie Smith's *St. Louis Blues* seems to the ear more basically blues than Mr. Handy's beautiful song in other interpretations, you have to go beyond counting bars and consider, for example, technique and tonality, evidence of scalar simplicity, etc.) In country singing of the kind Bill Broonzy's style grew out of, the four-bar blues line has various uses outside of blues. In far-flung areas of the South, in the present century and even to some extent still, songs, including variants of the four-bar blues line, were used for lining track, cutting cane, a chain gang chant or a lonely call. In blues adaptation a field holler or an old English ballad could be grist to the mill but there is no sure evidence that one form grew out of another. Within the memory of the oldest singers, these forms, and many others, existed simultaneously in the richest and most resourceful folk music this country has ever known.

Bill's first instrument was a home-made violin. He also played mandolin at one time. But it is difficult to think of him without his guitar, the cutting, slicing chords, the growling thunder of repeated phrases or, again, *stacatto*, almost stop-time, accents, or plaintive sounds, lightly brushing the harmony with rhythm. Not that he neglects the traditional blues relationship, in which the guitar sings out answering phrases, a second voice, but that he adds to it so much else that his guitar style becomes more complex than it sounds! Often he plays solo guitar, as he did for dancers—whether fiddle or guitar, the goal was the same—"If we played and sang loud enough," he tells us (text), "then we could stop singing and just hit on the strings and say to them: 'Rock, children, rock,' and they would rock all night long. That's how I learned to play guitar and not sing, and I got so that I could play four or five different styles without singing."

An aspect of blues and of Negro folk songs generally that was a basic influence on jazz may be traced to the accomodation of African singing styles to the conventions of West European music. The preoccupation of jazzmen with tonal centers seems to relate to this, as does the *stacatto-legato* phrasing—based on melodic phrasing in blues and which has its counterpart in the crowding or attenuation of lyric lines. These and other aspects of style testify to the close bonds between jazz and blues. Less tangible but no less a gift of Negro folk heritage has been the sense of wonder, of discovery and improvisation that added a fifth string to the banjo and as many lines to blues as there were places to sing them in.

"Young people have forgotten to cry the blues. Now they talk and get lawyers," said Big Bill. This remark, somewhat exaggerated, is intriguing in its suggestion of the role of music in changing environments. There were, to be sure, folk elements and a surprising amount of genuineness in rhythm and blues. Bill wasn't misled by the commercial overtones of such singers as Muddy Waters and Little Walter. Indeed, in his own first recorded blues, the verses are a mixture of the strong imagery typical of country blues and the commercial emphasis mentioned. These lines are from *Big Bill Blues*, quoted by Samuel B. Charters in "The Country Blues" (Rinehart):

> *Lord, my hair is a'raisin', my flesh begins to crawl*
> *I had a dream last night, babe, another mule in my*
> *doggone stall.*

"Bill copyrighted more than three hundred blues in his most active years," wrote Samuel B. Charters. "Many of them were almost taken from the recordings of the 1920's, and he probably would have had trouble defending his copyright in case of legal action, but some of the best, as *Keys To The Highway*, and *Looking Up At Down*, were Bill's own." It is obvious that a lot of horse-trading went on among singers, copyrights notwithstanding. In an older folk environment songs existed, generally speaking, outside the framework of copyright laws, in a freer musical environment. It was this freedom of movement that the blues singers, in their free use of lyric lines and blues strains, helped to preserve. For example, because Jazz Gillum was first to record it, he was sometime erroneously credited with Big Bill's *Key To The Highway*. But this was truly a blues out of Bill's own past, a strain of song like a chant, words that have special significance to share-croppers but that reach us all. How, he was once asked, did he think of the lyrics? "I'd just try to make it fit, that's all. Like when I'm writin' a blues about walkin', *about gettin' away from where I am*—

> *"I got the key to the highway,*
> *Yes, I'm billed out and bound to go;*
> *I'm gonna leave—leave here runnin'*
> *Because walkin' is most too slow."*

Bill's songs are sometimes weak on chronology but strong on life:

> *Plow hand's been my name,*
> *Lord, for forty years or more . . .*
> *Every night I'm hollerin' 'Whoa!*
> *Gee! Get up! 'in my sleep.*

There is a reference to his work as a molder during World War II in *Black, Brown and White*, and a stanza in another blues related to a specific experience when a mixed group (Bill and

18

some friends) wanted to share some beer at a Lafayette, Indiana, bar:

> *I was in a place one night,*
> *They was all havin' fun,*
> *They was all buyin' beer and wine*
> *But they would not sell me none.*

When Bill got around to visiting Africa, which he did in the 1950's, he found that Africans and himself had more in common than ancestry. For instance, like Bill, they were fed up with being called "Boy" and were saying so in loud voices. They might have liked the way Bill handled two typical "Boy" situations (out of the countless ones in his lifetime). Once, on the way to visit his mother—she died in 1957 at 102—Bill swung his second-hand Cadillac into a filling station outside Little Rock. The attendant's manner was typical:

"Whose car is this, boy?"

"Man I work for," said Big Bill, grinning, "My boss."

On another occasion, as Studs Terkel waited on a Chicago street corner for Bill, a State senator came up. Bill arrived as they were talking and introductions were made. The senator turned to Studs: "So he's your boy, eh?"

"He's not my . . . ."

"That's right," Bill cut in. . "He may not look it; but he's my father."

The senator chuckled, uncertain how to take it. With a "So long, boy," he hared off down the block.

Studs turned to Bill and whatever he'd meant to say, didn't come out. For Bill was laughing. He was laughing loud enough to have it reach the senator, who was now near the end of the block —and who lacked only the data to interpret it. Somewhere along the way Bill re-worded lines he'd written in 1928, so that they now read:

> *When I was born into this world*
> *This is what happen to me—*
> *I was never called a man*
> *An' now I'm 'round fifty-three.*

At his best, Big Bill Broonzy is the apotheosis of the country blues singer, handling raw tonality boldly, shaping it to song as a sculptor shapes granite—part moan, part shout, and more than either. Built on the bedrock of a folk style with its still strong, dominant African influence, he makes free use of harsh and resonant timbres. His use of quaver is the secular counterpart of a melismatic (many notes to a syllable) way of singing in Negro church music. Rhythmic tension is in the way he sings as well as in manipulation of the beat. The guitar contributes so much to this and, in fact, to the musical presentation *in toto,* that something seems lost rather gained, when the accompaniment is made more complex, particularly when the latter adds up to that musical banality to which rhythm and blues all too often lends itself. On balance, though, one would not have it otherwise. It would mean missing not only the hilarious hootenannies and the ear-splitting experience of Big Bill playing electric guitar on a commercial blues date, but those many occasions that were delights of spontaneity for listeners as they had been for the men involved when Bill had sympathetic and enthusiastic support, both from folk and jazz artists. (Among these were Ranson Knowling, bass, and Washboard Sam, trumpeter Punch Miller and pianists Black Bob, Josh Altheimer and Albert Ammons.)

Is it surprising that a man, so much of whose life was spent in cities, should be master of country style? Not really. Bill would be what he is and sing as he does, with all that great talent, even without records and songbooks. "Broonzy's incentive for writing the blues," *The Negro Digest* observed, "stems from a deep and bitter memory of the days when he worked on the railroad and at levee camps in Arkansas, as well as the never-break-even days on the tenant farms of the South." The style, the songs, come to him from his own past, from associations with country singers and country music that began in childhood and continued unbroken until his death. Like any gifted folk singer he added to his repertoire whenever possible, from whatever source. But he was no green grocer adding to his stock— he was more like the planter, soaking the soil in its immemorial organics, crossing the seed without science but with country know-how. He was a country singer because he never left the country. This is what we learn in Bill's own words—from those entertaining and endearing documentaries on long-play records and most movingly, most warmly, in words written out laboriously for Yannick Bruynoghe to transcribe, in the pages of "Big Bill Blues."

The beginning of blues acceptance was not particularly auspicious. Even while W. C. Handy's concerts lent dignity and a new stature to the blues, and the people whose creation they were, commercial production of blues was being stepped up to appeal to the masses of Negroes newly moved to northern urban centers. You can pinpoint the beginnings of commercial blues at the period following World War I. Even granted the nightmare world that poverty, ignorance and segregation made inevitable in northern urban slums, there was an over-emphasis, in commercial blues, on the seamy side of life that blues in a folk environment, though dealing with harsh and violent facts of life, could never have achieved. (Later, there was to be a partial shading off into the innocuous sentiments of popular music, a process traced by Samuel B. Charters in "The Country Blues".) Strongly on the debit side, the commercial blues, and that means a good proportion of recorded blues from the 1920's on, helped to perpetuate myths about Negroes, no longer in simulating a special image but in emphasizing characteristics and characters that could be proved out in particular instances but were, as is normal in shifting patterns of prejudice, accepted as typical.

"When record collectors would play one of the old records," Samuel B. Charters noted ("The Country Blues"), "complete with bleating saxophones, thundering piano and dirty lyrics, for one of Bill's new adolescent fans, there would be a moment of stunned silence and the new enthusiast would finally state in a serious tone, 'That's not the same Big Bill. There must be two men using the same name.'" But there weren't and it was.

The commercial blues did not, like the "coon song" with its minstrel-spawned stereo-type, its out-of-focus caricature, "sell" an image. Negroes, more than had been the case with "coon songs", made up the bulk of the audience for this new phase of popular entertainment. Commercial blues endeavored to be salacious and shocking while avoiding the socially offensive racialism of "coon songs". Not that they didn't give it a good try.

What is vulgarity? When one singer sang about her empty bed and made it hilarious, if somewhat obscure to that old lady in Dubuque, it behooved the dirtiest dead-end off Tin Pan Alley to grind out a wearisome procession of empty beds, with road maps. But new days were coming. For all the unbelievable horrors of bad taste and bad song-writing in commercial blues— Bill and his friends helped to perpetrate and perpetuate many of them — the vivid, exciting picture of real people living real lives, kept coming through.

Friends in Chicago, the interlude at Iowa State and, finally, the European tour (1951) arranged for him by Hugues Panassie— all helped to give back to Bill Broonzy his reason for singing. A second tour was again both a personal triumph and confirmation of the universal appeal of blues. How did they know what he was singing about? "A cry's a cry in any language . . . A shout's a shout, too, in any language."

Writing in *Melody Maker* (London, 8/23/58) of Bill's first London concert, at Kingsway Hall, 1951, Max Jones noted, "He found there an audience receptive to the best songs in his extensive repertoire and to his finest feats of guitarmanship, an audience that regarded him as a combination of creative artist and living legend . . . The voice was a shade less powerful than I had guessed it to be from American records (not one has been issued here)*. But it possessed all the strength and virility it needed for the toughest blues; and Bill displayed flexibility, inventiveness and all expressive range far beyond anything I expected. Other surprises were the immense sound and swing of the guitar playing, the dexterity revealed in solos, the richness of the accompaniment, and the wonderful relationship between vocal and instrumental parts . . . In Britain he played a significant part in building up a relatively large audience for blues and folk-song."

In the same issue of *Melody Maker*, Humphrey Littleton, the well known jazz trumpeter and band leader, made this interesting observation: "Big Bill was a difficult man to accompany, except on the rare occasions when he sang a conventional twelve-bar blues . . . He was sensitive to the jibes of the schooled players to know him very well in 1953 — we were both in Paris — and yet, by the book their arguments were convincing. By the standards of the more sophisticated 'modern' blues, his chords were 'wrong' and his measure erratic."

"I was the first one to welcome Bill in Europe," Yannick Bruynoghe wrote (in a letter to the author). Bruynoghe lives in Brussels where he edits a jazz magazine. "That was July, 1951. Panassie had arranged it, for the Hot Club of France, but Bill took a plane to Brussels and I went to greet him there. Of course, I was thrilled by his wonderful personality. I really came to know him very well in 1953— we were both in Paris — and it was then I persuaded him to write. He was quite enthusiastic about it . . . I'm glad to insist on the fact that there has been no tape-recorder used, such as the publicity mentioned. Bill was writing himself most of the things. Of course, I had to work a lot on all that — putting things together, changing some, dropping some pieces, etc. I also translated it into French. The main thing, in my idea, was to preserve his originality, his way of talking, even his accent." The results, (as I noted in my review of the book in the *New York Times*) were very much worth the effort.

You'd have thought Bill would have had it easier in the 1950's —a singer known and respected from Africa to the Argentine, perhaps better known in Australia than in Alabama — but this was not always the case. During rough spots he worked at odd jobs, such as a stint of janitor work at Hull House. Probably the sweetest "job" he had was at Circle Pines, a summer camp in Michigan. Bill did some work around the kitchen, but mostly he sang. It was a camp of kids and families both, a sort of folk song camp. Bill loved it there.

Was Bill accepted as a great singer by his own people, that is, the people who lived on the South Side, in Chicago? We have already seen how the young reacted, making a show of their rejection. This must have been more of a personal disappointment than he made out, yet he was able to speak of it with insight: "I don't blame them; it's like clothes, you can't expect people to like the same styles all the time."

Since Bill had been living far from Arkansas for many years, his stature as a country blues singer was once brought into question on this point alone. "If that wasn't country blues," Studs commented scornfully, "then all the Negroes who came up to Chicago from the Deep South and heard Bill sing at those taverns from Silvio's to Smitty's Corner, to Martin's Corner must have been wrong. I'm talking of the older people who brought the South up with them . . . There was a spirit of bonhomie such as I've seldom seen. Laughter of the kind you seldom hear. And Bill was the king."

"The first blues he ever heard," Studs reminded readers of his tribute to Bill Broonzy (*Saga*, Oct., 1961), "concerned the big flood of 1893. It was called *Cryin' Joe Turner*. On special occasions he'd sing it, like the time of his last weekend as a singer. He knew he might not have the chance again. He was entering the hospital the following Monday. There was a hush in the recording control room as he re-tuned his guitar. As soon as he touched the strings, we knew it was like no guitar we had ever heard before. It was a human voice, not just one but a whole ramshackle town. Bill was talking, a simple narrative about a flood, people losing homes, crops, everything. Joe Turner comes along. He's really two men, a white and a black. He helps out. 'And they would start cryin' and singin' this song.' The chord went *whang!* It was crying all right."

23

They tell me Joe Turner been here and gone,
Lord, they tell me Joe Turner been here and gone.

This is in sharp contrast to another blues in which Joe Turner is a figure of menace, the high sheriff or his deputy, who takes his man and is gone. The traditional refrain (as quoted, for example, in "The Art of Folk-Blues Guitar," an Oak Publication by Jerry Silverman) is similar. How it became part of different songs and developed differently in various parts of the South, will have to remain a mystery, one of many in the story of folk song growth.

The melody, like the legend, probably goes back to slavery days. And what an appropriate real-life characterization for a legend, the black man-white man! Out of this Bill created a great blues, expressing in human terms the tragedy of the slave society and that of segregation that succeeded it—an ingenuous and appealing symbolism, the black man on a mule going down the road too little traveled, to the rich heartland of common sharings, of hopes and hungers.

By July, 1958, Bill was a very sick man. In that month he wrote Dave Stevens who— with Lonnie Donnegan, Chris Barber and other friends in England — had planned a benefit concert for him: "Please don't think hard of me for not writing you all. I can't see, I am almost blind and my mind is not so good. I am so nervous . . . " The benefit concert realized more than five hundred pounds but before it could be allocated for Bill's use his widow, Mrs. Ruth Broonzy, cabled them the news of his death from cancer.

Big Bill Broonzy died at 5:30 a.m., August 14, 1958. On the 17th services were held at the big chapel of Chicago's Metropolitan Funeral Parlor. Memphis Slim, one of Bill's oldest friends, was on tour and couldn't be present but such of his friends as were in Chicago paid their respects and Studs Terkel, writing later in *Saga*, speculated on some of their thought: Mahalia Jackson, singing *Just A Closer Walk With Thee* — perhaps she recalled Big Bill as he ambled into her sick room in a Paris hospital, held her hand and joshed. Brother John Sellers, singing *Nobody Knows The Trouble I've Seen* — did he think of the early, lonely days when he came north from Clarksdale, Mississippi, and Big Bill was there, helping to ease the way? "And what of Memphis Slim on that August day?" Somewhere in southern Illinois, singing songs, his own and Bill's and others, to strangers.

The pallbearers tossed white gloves on the lowered casket at Lincoln Cemetery:

"Tampa Red? Gypped, euchered and triple-crossed by song agents, promoters and hot-shot takers — as have been all of Bill's friends at one time or another and none more than Bill himself— was he remembering . . . 'Watch those guys, get it on the dotted line, but read it careful first and don't be too fast in puttin' down John Henry an' if the print's too small get a magnifyin' glass.'?"

"Sunnyland Slim? 'Bill was closer to me than a brother.'" Sunnyland, who works on a truck of the Sanitation Department, who still sings his fine blues when he can.

"Muddy Waters?" For all his spectacular singing in rhythm and blues, he kept the real blues. In his voice and in his songs, some of which came from older singers like Big Bill.

"Little Walter? The young wild harmonica blower from Alexandria, Louisiana. When in 1938, a small kid, fresh and wide-eyed from the Deep South, he sneaked into a rough-and-tumble Chicago tavern, who was it among those tall men who encouraged him and taught him so many songs?"

"J. B. Lenoir? Red Nelson? Little Brother Montgomery? Jasper Taylor? Guitar men, piano men. Each retained his own piece of Bill as the dirt was shoveled onto the box."

And what of the others, that day?

"Lil Armstrong, tiny and vital, sat in that chapel, too. And Bill's twin sister, all the way from Little Rock. And Rose, his gentle, moaning widow. And all the little girls and little boys, white and black, who had come to love this man during his last years."

Acknowledgements: Studs Terkel, for his letters and for permission to quote from his article. Institute for Jazz Studies.

Books: Recent books on blues, in addition to those mentioned in text, include Jerry Silverman's "Folk Blues" (MacMillan); LeRoi Jones' "Blues People" (Morrow); and Paul Oliver's "Blues Fell This Morning" (Horizon). Negro folk music and backgrounds: Harold Courlander's "Negro Folk Music, U. S. A." (Columbia U. Press.)

(*This situation has changed — fans overseas have access to several albums, including the Folkways sets, and to special collections of the commercial blues period. The latter are discussed in a fascinating article in the English *Jazz Monthly* (April, 1960) G. E. Lambert's *"Your Game is Too Strong, Mama"*.

My Life

THE reason I'm writing this book is because I think that everybody would like to know the real truth about Negroes singing and playing in Mississippi. I'm one of the oldest still alive and I want everybody to know that we Mississippi musicians care just as much about our way of singing and playing as anyone else, although we know we's not the only Southern peoples that sing and play the blues.

But I can say, for Mississippi and Arkansas, we are proud of our way of singing and playing the blues. I know Arkansas and Mississippi because I have lived in them two States all of my life.

I was born in Mississippi and was partly raised in Arkansas and I travelled from Mississippi to Arkansas until I got to be fifty years old and I still go down to visit my people in Mississippi and Arkansas and I still love my home-town in the South.

Of course we know that it ain't just Negroes that play and sing the blues because there's some hillbillies and cowboys that sing the blues, too. They sing it their way and we sing our way, we know and love our way and they know and love their way. The hillbillies isn't ashamed to play their old style, so why should we be ashamed of the way we learned to play and sing the blues?

Nobody gave us lessons, it was just born in us to sing and play the blues.

Some Negroes tell me that the old style of blues is carrying Negroes back to the horse-and-buggy days and back to slavery—and who wants to be reminded of slavery?—and some will say this ain't slavery no more, so why don't you learn to play something else? I just tell them I can't play nothing else and they say to me:

'You should learn, go and take lessons and learn to play real music.'

Then I will ask them:

'Ain't the blues real music?'

All they can and will say to me:

'Not the way you play and sing about mules, cotton, corn, levee camps and gang songs. Them days, Big Bill, is gone for ever.'

'Oh no,' I'll answer. 'You sure is wrong. Look at some of your clothes, they's still raising cotton, and there is still mules and gangs in America, and so as long as the South grows cotton and mules and men eat cornbread, men and women is still going to give each other the blues, because everywhere I go in the USA they sing the blues.'

And that reminds me about one day me and my Uncle went fishing. We didn't catch no fish but we caught a big turtle, we drug him home and my Uncle told me to make him stick his neck out of his shell. I tucked a stick and put it in front of him. The turtle caught hold of the stick and wouldn't turn it loose. So my Uncle said:

'Hold his head right there and I'll cut it off.'

My Uncle took the axe and cut the turtle's head off and we went in the house and stayed there a while. When we came back, no turtle. So we looked for him and the turtle was nearly back to the lake where we caught him. We picked him up, brought him back to the house and my Uncle said:

'There's a turtle who's dead and don't know it.'

And that's the way a lot of people is today: they got the blues and don't know it.

And there are lots of reasons for me to write about the blues. Because I know the blues and love it. I don't care how it is played or sung and I don't care who plays or sings them, a black man or a white man, if they sing their way or my way. I know there ain't but a small amount of the real blues singers still living and in none of the places where I've been there is somebody giving lessons about how to play the old-time and Down-South blues. Even the people in the South are learning to play fast time and jump, the young people like to jitterbug, and if I was to stop playing the real old slow blues I don't know what would become of it.

I don't want the old blues to die because if they do I'll be dead, too, because that's the only kind I can play and sing and I love the old style.

I have travelled all over the USA, in every State and also in Mexico, Spain, Germany, England, Holland, Switzerland, Italy, Africa, Belgium, France, trying to keep the old-time blues alive, and I'm going to keep on as long as Big Bill is still living.

On my father's side he had four brothers and one sister. His mother was a mulatto coloured woman. Her family throwed her out when she married my grandfather, because he was real black.

I remember when I was big enough I had to walk my grandmother to church and sit outside the gate and wait until the church meeting was over and take her home. The reason I had to sit outside was because they didn't allow black Negroes in their churches and schools.

My father told me how he met my mother in slave time. He said they had to pick so much cotton a day and she didn't get her task done and he'd seen her get a lashing, and after that he said he would pick cotton fast to get his task done and crawl through the grass and weed and help her, and he did that every day.

So when they was freed and sent back to their home they found out that both lived in Baton-Rouge, Louisiana, and they got married.

Often I have heard my mother say:

'Any time a man takes a chance on his life to help me, he's good enough for me to marry and have a baby for.'

And she did so: she had twenty-one babies. I believe it because I've seen sixteen of them and they all's still alive. She said the others was born dead, three of them, and two lived to get two years old. She said it was because she had to help my father haul wood and cut down trees and plough the crops.

My mother had two twin boys and a girl-and-a-boy twins. That boy is Bill.

My mother had ten sisters and one brother. My father had six children by another woman, but my mother just found that out after he died. If she had known about that he might have died earlier.

My father was a good old man. He died in 1930, and he always said to me:

'Do you know you's thirty minutes younger than your sister?'

I'd say, 'Yessir.'

He used to say 'You came into this world behind a woman and you'll always be behind them.'

So it must be true because I'm fifty-nine years old and have to wear glasses, but I still like to see them beautiful mileposters, better known as legs, and big ones of course.

A lot of peoples think that the Negroes from the South and born in Mississippi don't know how old they is. But that's wrong: my mother and father can't forget the year I was born because there was a terrible flood in 1892 and I was born in 1893.*And not only that: there was two of us born the same day, me and my twin sister.

Most of the Negroes was born when something had happened the year before or the year after or the same year.

And in the slavery time they had the same way of keeping up with the date of the kid's birthday and they would cook an ash cake or roast some sweet potatoes or they all would go hunting.

In them times every year something strange would happen—a drought, a flood or a picnic, or some Negro would get killed in some strange way, and so you see you can't forget when your child was born in the South. If you had ever been in a flood or a storm over there, or if you could have been at one of our camp meetings or our big picnics where everything was free, you wouldn't never forget it.

That's the way we know the year we was born, and after we get twelve or fifteen years old we keep giving big feasts and that day we call it our birthday and we would have fun.

When I was seven years old I was hired out to work for a man by my father and the man had six children: four boys and two girls.

My job was to take care of all of them. Two of the boys was older than me. The older boy went to college and when he came back he was a lawyer; the next boy went to college and when he came back he was a doctor; then the two girls went to college and when they came back they was school teachers; then the younger boy went to college and when he came back he took over his father's place and ran it for him.

I started to work for this man in 1899 and I worked for him till 1916 and ever since I'd seen all of them go to college I'd been wanting to go to college, too, because every one of

*See introduction

the six children went to college, came back and got to be
something.

So in 1917 I was called to the army and I came back home
in 1919 and I had learned a lot but I still wanted to go to
college and I didn't get to go all that time from 1900.

I learned to play music and learned how to work and how
to preach and learned how to sing the blues and how to sing
Negro church songs, but I still wanted to go to college.

So I got to go to college in 1950 and I got Doctor Shelleter
and Mr Pemburg to thank for that: they was the cause of
my dream to come true.

They got me a job as a janitor in the Iowa State College
and I'm happy and I thank them for that.

When I was about ten years old I made a fiddle out of a
cigar box, a guitar out of goods boxes for my buddy Louis
Carter, and we would play for the white peoples' picnics and
some time they would have two stages. Negroes would be on
one.side and the Whites on the other.

The white peoples liked to hear us play our old-time songs
and one white man named Mister Mack, he came up to me.

'Bill,' he said, 'you and Louie is too good Negro fiddle
players to be playing them old home-made fiddles, so I'm
going to buy you all some brand new ones.'

So he did. But when they came I couldn't play either one
of them, so Louie cried because he couldn't play his guitar.
But I talked to him and we had to put them back in their
boxes and play the old ones.

One of the meanest white men came up and said:

'Them Negroes can't play no real fiddles. Give them their
old cigar boxes and make them play them all night or till we
get tired and ready to go home.'

When they let us go home a white man, the one that
bought the new fiddles for us, he said:

'You-all come with me and get your fiddles and take them home and keep them until you can learn to play them.'

So we did, but it taken me and Louie about three months to learn how to play them.

So I started to preaching and I preached for four years, and then I went back to playing again, both me and Louie. I had been a preacher and Louie was a deacon at the same time.

So we both went back to playing and we was the best two Negro musicians around there. That's what the white people said. We would be playing and sitting under screened porches while the other Negroes had to work in the hot sun and the white peoples called us 'their Negroes' and thought we was too good to work with the other Negroes. Of course we didn't get no money, we got all we wanted to eat and a lot of old clothes they gave us.

This is the reason why I stopped preaching and went back to playing the fiddle: one day I was sitting astride on a fence and my Uncle came up to me and said:

'That's the way you's living: straddle the fence,' he said. 'Get on one side or the other of the fence.'

That's what he said and he meant preach or play the fiddle, one at the time. Don't try to be both at the same time. Just be what you are: a preacher *or* a fiddler.

So I went to bed that night and thought it over. I said to myself: 'I can't read or write, and I'm trying to lead people and tell them the right way and don't know how and what is right myself.'

So I went to the field the next day, my wife came out to bring me some water, I stopped to drink it and the man I was working for came out there and said, 'Bill,' and I answer, 'Sir.'

'Bill, I want you to play the fiddle for a four-day picnic.'
I said to him:

'I'm a preacher.'

'The hell with that preachin',' he said. 'Here's fifty dollars, and you be sure to be there. There will be a new fiddle waiting for you and a guitar for Louie.'

So my wife took the fifty dollars and put it in her stocking and said to me:

'This is more money than we've ever had and you'd better play that fiddle and play like you never did before because out of all your preachin' you haven't never brought no money home.' So she said:

'I'm going to town tomorrow and spend this, so Mister Mack can't take it back and you know what that means, don't you, Bill . . .?'

'Yeah, that means I'd better play, or run away and leave you and my baby.'

'Yes, or lose your wife,' she said.

So I played those four days and nights.

Superstitious Negroes don't walk under ladders, don't sing in bed, watch the number 13, don't eat the last biscuit on the table. If two people are walking together, don't let another man or woman walk between you, don't let a black man or woman in your house on Monday morning and don't pay no bill you owe on Monday; don't do no kind of work on Sunday unless you say: 'The ox is in the mere and I've got to pull him out,' then it's all right to do any kind of work, and don't sew a button on your clothes exactly where it was unless you put a stick in your mouth. If a snake has crossed the road and left a track, turn around and go back, or if you can tell which way he was going and can tell that he hasn't been long across, try to go around in front of him— many times I've went two or three miles out of my way to try to cut a snake; if you kill a snake don't turn his billy up because if you do it will rain before sundown.

I remember once in 1918 I was in the army and six of us had a pass to go to town and at the same time some white soldiers was going to town, too.

There was two camps there: the one for Negroes on one side of the road and the white camp on the other.

When we came to the edge of the town, a black cat started across the street and one Negro said:

'Look that damn' black cat, don't let him cross us, it's bad luck.'

So we six Negroes started running to cut the cat who ran into the doorway of a store and we ran in there, trying to catch him and hollering:

'Catch that black cat, don't let him cross!'

There was twelve white soldiers standing there, looking at us and laughing, and this lasted for about two hours, so we finally catched the cat and carried him back to the side of the street where he was coming from, and we turned him loose.

One of the white soldiers said to another:

'Let's go back to camp, that's enough fun for tonight, seeing six black soldiers catching one black cat.'

So the white soldiers went back and we went to town, got some drinks and returned to camp, laughing. We did not hurt the cat, but all of us had scratched legs, arms and heads.

From then on, every time a white soldier would see a black one, he would start to laugh.

One day, we all was sitting out beside the road looking at the white soldiers having exercise, and they couldn't do nothing but laugh at us. We all got mad because we thought they was laughing at us because we was black and they was white. We all walked across the road. One officer met us and said:

'What's wrong, soldiers?'

'What is you all laughing about?' we asked.

'I don't know,' the officer said, 'but I'll sure find out.'

He called the lieutenant. By that time there was about two hundred black soldiers who had crossed the road and all our officers had came over. They told us to sit down and wait until they found out why the white soldiers was laughing.

The officer came back with twelve of the white soldiers, the same who was with us that night we had catched the black cat.

By that time there was over a thousand soldiers there.

So they put one of these soldiers up on a big box and told him:

'Tell the black soldiers why you all was laughing.'

So he started to tell the story about six black soldiers catching one black cat and when he got through everybody was laughing, even the general.

And we all went to our places and some started shooting dice or playing cards.

After that day, the white soldiers would come over and play games with us and for fourteen months everybody laughed about that night when we had catched the black cat.

Once my Uncle and another man named John was leaving Arkansas, going back to Mississippi. Everybody down there would halt the Negroes when they would leave from one State and going to another because they would steal hogs in Arkansas and take them back to Mississippi. So when they would go to cross the State line the highway police would search them.

So my Uncle Jerry and his friend John was riding in an old one-seater Ford car and the police stood on the road and my Uncle had seen them about a mile away.

'There's the police,' he said to John. 'What is we gonna

do with this hog?'

'Put your coat around him,' said John, 'and put your hat on his head.'

So Jerry did and when they got up to the police they was stopped.

'What's your name?' asked the police.

'John.'

'And you, what's your name?'

'Jerry.'

'OK,' said the police, 'go on through, you boys look to be all right.'

So they started off.

'Wait a minute,' said the police. 'What did you say your name was?'

He said: 'Jerry.'

'And what is your name?'

'John,' he said.

'And you there in the middle?' asked the police.

The hog with the hat and coat on didn't say anything, so the police pushed him in the side with the stick he was carrying, and the hog grunted.

'You two boys is all right,' said the police, 'but that Negro in the middle, the grunting Negro, he's about the ugliest Negro I've ever seen in my life.'

And the police told them to get that ugly Negro away from there, so they drove away with the hog with his hat and coat on and carried him home.

It would be bad if they caught you stealing a hog. They would give you two years on the farm and a hundred dollars fine.

That time they got away with the hog by putting their coat and hat on him. Of course he was a black hog and the police thought that he was just an uglier Negro and they called him the old grunting Negro.

I've known a white man who lived in Arkansas and who's name was Crack White. He had a plantation about twenty-five miles wide, he had a white fence around his place, all of his chickens, ducks, turkeys, geese, horses, cows, hogs, goats, sheep, dogs, cats and everything on his place was white. He even had the trees painted white and all his wagons and farm tools, too.

That man didn't like nothing black. He didn't like Negroes at all and every time one of his chickens would hatch off a black chicken he would give it away to a Negro.

So one day I was passing by his farm and one of his horses had had a colt. He said to me:

'Say, boy, do you want a little horse to raise?'

'Yeah, sure.'

So he gave him to me and one of his cows had a black calf and he gave him to me, too.

Every day some Negro would drive his wagon by Mr White's farm and get something black.

About two years later the State put a highway across his place and he told them:

'It's all right to put that road across my place, but I'm gonna put signs "No Negroes allowed through here".'

And he did. So we said:

'He's good to us, we haven't been going across his place, so we won't now. Of course it's five miles farther, but it's all right.'

And we all went around his place. But every year, when he would go to gather his fruits he would have too much and he would have his peoples that worked for him (all of them was white, of course) to load up the wagons and bring all kinds of fruits in the Negro neighbourhood and just dump them on the ground. Some time they would dump four wagon loads every day and we would have a free picnic and he would give hogs, cows, goats, sheep, chicken and everything.

But he didn't allow us to thank him for nothing he did for us, because he didn't like a Negro and didn't take nothing from a Negro, not even a thank-you.

A lot of people say 'a dollar is your best friend' and 'a dollar in hand trust no man'.

But I remember once, when I was touring over France, I had 200 US dollars, 50,000 French francs in my pocket, and I would have starved to death if it hadn't been for three French boys that was my friends: Pépé, Guy Lafitte and Hadjo.[1] Because nobody in the town I was playing could speak English at all and I couldn't speak a word of French. I couldn't ask for water or bread.

In the North of Arkansas some other time I had money in my pocket and I was put off a train in a town where they didn't allow Negroes. I had to walk about five miles and I passed four or five stores. Peoples was in but when I would ask for food they'd say to me: 'Negro read and run. If you can't read, run anyway.' I did that and I ran to a water tank where the trains stop to take water, and there was a man there to take care of the place and give the trains water when they stop.

He saw me and said:

'Where's you trying to go to?'

'I'm trying to find something to eat and get home,' I told him.

So he put me in a big box and locked it up. I could hear some white men asking him did he see a Negro pass here.

'Yes,' he said, 'he went that way.'

So they left and he came back to the box and gave me his dinner pail and told me to stay in that box until he would come for me.

---

[1] Pianist André Persiany, tenor sax Guy Lafitte and bass player Hadjo accompanied Big Bill for a concert tour in France during the summer of 1951.

I stayed in that box for two days and nights and he would come by and unlock the box and give me fresh water and food and let me get out and go to the toilet when there wasn't anybody around. He told me he was taught not to like Negroes, but I was one Negro he thought that really needed a friend and he said:

'You's harmless, you's not trying to hurt anybody or trying to steal or break in no place or trying to undermine nobody for his job. You just wanted to eat and get home, just like my son or anyone else that might make a mistake in his life, so why should I let my peoples kill you? So I'm gonna help you but remember I don't want no pay for what I'm doing for you. I'm not allowed to take nothing from no Negro and I don't like no Negroes either.'

He said them words with tears in his eyes and when he put me in a box-car on the freight train that was going straight to my home, he gave me a box of food and a five-dollar bill and he said:

'Goodbye and good luck, old Negro, but don't never come back here again, because we don't like no Negroes in this part of the world.'

So you see I know a dollar don't mean everything to me. A good friend means more to Big Bill Broonzy than all the money in the world. Of course I've met some supposed-to-be friends with dollar signs for eyes and I got fooled and got beat out of money and they lied to me in all kind of ways. But what I mean is a real friend, and I happily got some of them in Europe and in the USA.

Does every blues singer and every jazz musician drink whisky and does every bop musician smoke weeds? And what do some of our USA preachers, doctors, lawyers and policemen do? Oh well, it wouldn't be so bad if it was free to do some of these things and not a crime.

I do remember one day that me and a friend was in a basement flat and had just drunk a fifth of whisky. As we came out there was a man coming down the street, staggering, bothering nobody, just trying to make it home with his load. So this friend of mine looks at the man and tells me:

'Fellows like that should be put off the street and in jail.'

'What about me and you?' I said, 'We's on the street, too, you know.'

'But that man has been drinking wine.'

'What's the difference? We's just as drunk as he is. He's drunk of wine and we's of whisky. The pot can't call the kettle black. A drunk is just a drunk. I don't care how or why you get drunk, or if it's in a fine hotel or in the basement, in slums, on a farm or on Wall Street. What's the difference? Maybe you'll act better, but you's still drunk.'

So he agreed. We walked on, stopped in another basement and had another bottle. Then we went to our club meeting.

So this is what I want to say: if you's a jazz musician, a bopper or a blues player and singer, think twice before you say anything about so-and-so, about how he plays or sings and how he gets his kicks (better known as how he gets drunk). Think first: 'What do I smoke or drink, and am I making the right notes and chords all the time or not?'

And you won't have time to talk about no one else.

About musicians that drink or use dope of some kind, I have tried it all but for me it's alcohol because I started out on moonshine whisky and marijuana don't do nothing to me.

I do believe that all musicians get used to something because he or she is nervous just as anyone else that uses tobacco, cigarettes, cigars, chews or dips snuff; they get nervous and they smoke, chew or dip more than ever.

Some of the younger musicians use it because he or she is playing the same type of music or sing the same songs as some famous artist. They hear and they read about that artist using dope or drinking whisky and they can play and sing good, so they copy after them and they start drinking or using dope and they get in a habit of every time they play or sing to get the one or the other.

I do know that every time since I've been playing and singing the blues I can't think of my own songs until I get about two or three good drinks. Then all the songs I ever sang come back to me and it drives away all fear. I've been playing and singing in public ever since 1912 and even today I get a little shake when I first go on a stage, so I always take a little drink before I go on.

I remember once I got a job in New York City, playing and singing the blues, and the boss told me that I couldn't drink if I was playing for him. So I didn't drink for two weeks because I would lose my job if I was caught.

One day I went to meet some friends at a place and had plenty whisky to drink there. I got drunk and had to play that night at ten o'clock.

When I got to the place I just could see the boss and I knew I had lost my job because he could tell I was drunk. The place was packed with peoples and I went to the boss and told him:

'I'm drunk. Please forgive me. It'll never happen again.'

He looked at me and walked off. So I played the two shows that night and went for my pay. The boss gave me five dollars more than usual.

'Take this,' he said, 'and be drunk tomorrow night. You played better tonight than ever.'

So every night he would come to my dressing room and smell my breath, go out and send me a big glass of whisky before I started to sing.

I don't need whisky all the time; just when I have to play and sing it helps me out.

A man told me once about Albert:

'Albert Brand is cooked from drinking so much whisky,' he said, 'and he's going to die soon.'

That man who told me that about Albert, he had never taken a drink in his life, he said, and it was only six months difference in the two men's deaths. So I think everybody dies from something. I do know everybody has heart trouble, because if nothing goes wrong with your heart and it don't stop beating you'll never die.

But I do say that I would rather hire a musician that uses marijuana than one that drinks whisky. I found out in all five bands I've been the leader of, that a tea smoker is not nosy and don't forget his music and isn't hard to get along with and he always wants to try to learn something new and to improve old songs.

A musician who drinks whisky he either talks too much, won't listen to his leader and the way he plays tonight he'll play in a different key tomorrow night or start an argument and won't play at all. I know I've had them in the studio getting behind a piano and falling asleep. Many times I've taken seven musicians to the studio to make records and I had to finish with three because four of them got drunk and bawled me out.

'That ain't the way that blues go!'

They would tell me that and I had written the song myself.

I remember once we all went about fifty miles out of town to make records and when we got to the studio I called all the musicians and said:

'Let's go over some of the songs.'

So they all got ready but one, the trumpet player.

'What's wrong?' I asked.

'I got my case,' he said, 'but no trumpet in it.'

So I had to go and rent one.

He was a whisky head.

What is a blues singer, a good one or a bad one? I say he's just a meal ticket for the man or woman who wears dollar-signs for eyes.

I remember the first time I went to see Mr Mayo Williams in 1922. He told me I couldn't play good enough. But he did like my playing, so I went back home and told John Thomas, who was my pal, and he said: 'OK, I'll go down there with you.'

So he did and Mr Williams asked me how many songs did I know and could I sing. I told him four songs: *House Rent Stomp*, *Big Bill Blues*, *Gonna Tear It Down* and *Tod Pail Blues*.

'All right,' Mr Williams said. 'You practise on them and come back in about two weeks.'

So I did every night, me and Thomas, and we went back. Mr Williams let me make two songs: *Big Bill Blues* and *House Rent Stomp*.

That was in 1923. In the same year I made the other two which was never released on record by me but was made by other artists, maybe after my first visit for tryout, and since that time *Gonna Tear It Down* was played by several bands.

I got no money for them two songs, and for the two first ones John Thomas told a lie and got a hundred dollars. He told them his father had just died and that it would take a hundred dollars to bury him. But I know that Thomas's father had died when he was twelve years old. I didn't tell no lie and I got fifty dollars, and that's all I got because they told me that I had broken one of the recording machines which cost five hundred dollars by patting my feet on it.

So I got nothing out of those two songs. They came out on October the 25th and I bought every one I found that was for sale. There was two places on Maxwell Street in Chicago. I would go to one and Thomas to the other, and we did that every day. That's how I know that they sold good, because we two alone bought fifty of them.

Me and Thomas was sitting down, talking about what we had to do to make a record. They had my head in a horn of some kind and I had to pull my head out of the horn to read the words and back in it to sing. And they had Thomas put on a pillar about two feet high and they kept on telling us to play like we would if we was at home or at a party, and they kept on telling us to relax and giving us moonshine whisky to drink—and I got drunk.

I went to sleep after the recording and when I woke up, on the way home, John Thomas told me that I had signed some paper. I told him I hadn't.

'Look in your jumper pocket,' he said.

And sure enough there the paper was, signed with ink.

'You've let them make you drunk,' Thomas said, 'and you've signed our rights away.'

And that's what I had done. All I could do was cry and tell him how sorry I was. And when he told the lie and got a hundred dollars I couldn't say anything but: 'Yes, Mister Williams, Thomas's daddy did die last night at about ten o'clock.'

So Thomas got the money and stayed hiding around for two weeks. Mr Williams told me to get Thomas and bring him down to his office, but I had to tell him that Thomas hadn't come back from burying his father.

Mr Williams asked me to bring Thomas down there as soon as he came back to town. After two weeks I saw Thomas and we went to Williams's office every day for about a week and he was so busy that we couldn't see him at all.

'The heck with him,' Thomas said, 'I don't want to go down there no more.'

The next time I saw Mr Williams, me and James Williams and Paul Bennet went to make records. James played piano,

I played guitar and Paul sang two sides. That was in 1926. Paul got ten dollars, I got fifteen dollars and James got twenty-five.

Later on, in 1928, I met Mr Lester Melrose. I was a grocery boy and he told me to come to his office. So I did and carried my guitar with me. Him and his buddy Herman took me to the studios and I made four songs for them: *Date With An Angel Blues*, *The Walking Blues*, *Big Bill Blues No. 2* and *House Rent Stomp No. 2*.

About two months later I made *Bull Cow Blues*, *Milk Cow Blues*, *Serve It To Me Right Blues* and *Mama Let's Cuddle Some More*.

After that time I got a piano player, Black Bob, and I played with him for several years.

When we talk about big town blues, the words 'big town' is places like New Orleans, Memphis, Saint Louis, Kansas City, Atlanta, Houston, Little Rock, Jackson, Vicksburg, and that's where these big town blues players started playing.

They lived like a king because most of them had women cooking for some rich white man and they lived in the servants' house behind the white man's house.

These musicians was not seen in the day. They came out at night. His meal was brought out to him from the white man's house in a pan by his woman. We called them kind of men 'sweet back papas'.

Them men didn't know how cotton and corn and rice and sugar-cane grows and they didn't care. They went out, dressed up every night and some of them had three and four women. One fed him and the other bought his clothes and shoes. These is the men that wear ten-dollar Stetson hats and twenty-dollar gold pieces at their watch and diamonds in their teeth and on their fingers.

This kind of men caused women like Bessie Smith and her

sisters, Ma Rainey, Ida Cox, Memphis Minnie, Merline Johnson, Victoria Spivey, Lil Green and a lot of other women blues singers to sing the blues. The women get the blues from all the trouble those men give them, but these men don't have the blues, hell no.

So you know how these songs started, songs like *Me And My Chauffeur, Grave Digger Blues, See See Rider, King Size Papa, My Mellow Man, Deep Sea Diver, My Man Ain't Come Up To My House* and a lot more blues the women sang about how much they loved their sweet papa and what they done for them and how the man could love them.

If this man left one of the women and got another one and if she couldn't find him to kill him, she would sing about what she would like to do to him or what she would do to get him back.

I do remember one of these sweet back papas had a woman and if she didn't get enough money for him he would beat her up. So one night he told his woman to go out and don't come back till she got seven dollars.

So she went out and a policeman that they called Mr Six, he asked her: 'What is you doing out this time at night?'

'My husband told me to go out and don't come back till I got him seven dollars.'

'Come on,' said Six, 'I'll go home with you and you knock on the door.'

She knocked on the door, Big Six standing behind her.

Her husband hollered to her:

'Have you got that seven dollars?'

'No,' she said, 'but I got Six with me.'

So her husband thought she had six dollars, he opened the door and in stepped Big Six, the baddest Negro policeman Chicago has ever seen. He gave the sweet papa a good beating and took him to jail. So that's the song about *He's In The Jail House Now.*

My Songs

BLUES IN 1890
(Joe Turner Blues)[1]

This is a song that was sung in eighteen and ninety-two
There was a terrible flood that year
And the poor people cried and sang this song
To let everybody know how they felt
About a whole year's work and no pay
The droughts killed their crops and all their belongings
Their clothes and their livestock too
And the only man they knowed that could help them was Joe
  Turner
And Joe Turner was known to be a man that would help all
  poor people
The white and the black
And then they would start crying and singing this song:

(REFRAIN)
They tell me Joe Turner been here and gone
Lord, they tell me Joe Turner been here and gone
They tell me Joe Turner been here and gone

Then they would go out hunting rabbits, 'coons, 'possums
Anything they could catch to eat

---

[1] This blues is partly spoken and partly sung (the refrain). Big Bill tells the story and sings to a wonderful and original guitar background. Recorded in Paris, France, for *Vogue* Records (Nr. 131 or LP 030). Different versions are included in the following LP's: *Folkways* FG3586 and FA2326, *Verve* MG V-3000-5, Vol. 1.

Sometimes they would catch something
Then again they wouldn't catch anything
Then they would come home, look in their kitchens
They would find flour, meat and molasses
That Joe Turner had left there for them
Then they would know that Joe Turner had been there
And they would start crying and singing this song:

They tell me Joe Turner been here and gone
Lord, they tell me Joe Turner been here and gone
They tell me Joe Turner been here and gone

They knowed there wasn't nothing in their kitchen to eat when
   they left
And they knowed that Joe Turner had been there
And left food, clothes and everything for them
Then they would get happy, start shouting and dancing
Then they would do a little boogie-woogie too.

I recorded a blues titled *Blues in* 1890 which was sung and
played already three years before I was born. My Uncle and
his pal, Stonewall Jackson, they both played banjo and they
played and sang this song. It had no name at that time but
it was sung and played the same way that I do it today. The
only difference is that I play it on guitar.

My Uncle said that before they got the idea of making
them a banjo, when it rained or after they got off from their
work, they had nothing to make music on. They would sing
and pat their hands, and to get different sounds some would
pat their hands hard and some of them would rub their
hands together. When they sang, there would be a woman
between every two men, they would put a young man with
an old man and that was their bass and tenor, and an old
woman and a young girl together for their alto and soprano.

My Uncle was a blacksmith, fixing all the ploughs and the farmers' tools. All the different ploughs had different sizes of points on them. My Uncle had to keep them sharp and ready for ploughing. He said that one day he was sharpening them all and every time he would hit a different one it had a different sound, so he took one of each and hung them up with a piece of wire. He hitted from one to the other, singing at the same time, and he got a musical tone out of them.

One day he was fixing an old tub that they wash clothes in, he took a stick to knock the dirt out of the tub and he got another sound from that. So he would hit the tub slow and he would hit it fast, with one stick then with two sticks and he knew he had something there. He called Stonewall Jackson, who was his buddy, told him to hit the plough points and he would hit the tub. So they would do that every day when they got a chance.

Some other day my Uncle was at home and his wife told him to come and help her to clean the kitchen; she gave him a broom to sweep the floor. He said his hands were wet from washing dishes, he laid his hand on the table and pulled the broom handle across his finger and he got a sound; he noticed that when he would press hard on his finger with the broom handle the sound would be different, so he kept on changing his fingers different ways and he got different sounds.

He took the broom to the blacksmith shop and called Stonewall Jackson and another of his pals. This one got the stick to hit on the tub, Stonewall hitted on plough points and Uncle Jerry got the broom and his finger on the table and they did that for a long time. Every day or two they would get together and play and sing.

My Uncle said it rained one day and they couldn't work in the fields. They got their things together, started to play and everybody came to hear them play them plough points, broom handle and tub. Even the white people liked it and they played for the white people to dance. When they got tired they would leave and he told me they would have a ball drinking and eating what the white people had left—apple cider and barbecue pig.

One of the things they were doing was *Tell Me Joe Turner Been Here And Gone*. They couldn't sing that song when there was white people around because the white people wanted them to believe there was nobody who could treat the Negro no better than they could and did. But the Negro believed there was such a man as Joe Turner—it was their belief.

So when they would have trouble they would sing about Joe Turner. If they needed food or clothes or wanted it to rain so that their crops could grow, they would cry and sing *Tell Me Joe Turner Been Here And Gone*.

In 1892 there was a big flood and they lost everything they had and in 1893 it was a drought that killed everything they had planted on their farms.

They had no food or clothes and they would go hunting for rabbits, 'coons and 'possums and some would go fishing; some time they would catch no fish, no rabbits, 'coons or 'possums and they would come home and find meat, flour and molasses in their kitchens that Joe Turner had left there for them, and they would start to cry and sing *Tell Me Joe Turner Been Here and Gone*.

My Uncle told me when I was ten years old they would do a dance that they called the boogie-woogie. Some of them would go across the floor and the others would pat their hands and say, 'Oh let's boogie, children, because Joe Turner's sure good to us ain't he.' Everybody would woogie and say, 'Oh yes.' And they was happy and glad because they had food to eat, clothes and shoes to wear, that they had found in their homes what Joe Turner had left for them.

My Uncle Jerry told me there was a man who had about

fifty slaves. He had three bosses over these slaves—they called them slave-drivers. And this white man didn't allow his slave-drivers, who were white men too, to whip his slaves or to say bad words to them. The old white man had also an old Negro who told him everything that the other Negroes had done and where they went. His name was Joe. All the Negroes would go to old Joe to get the permission when they wanted to do something. So the first time they went out hunting and found food and clothes in their home when they came back, they went to old Joe:

'We left home this morning, came back now and there's food and clothes in our home. We wonder who put it there, Joe?'

Old Joe would say: 'Oh well, it's Joe Turner who left it there.' And he would start humming this tune, *Tell Me Joe Turner Been Here And Gone.* And they all would sing it with old Joe and old Joe would disappear.

This old man that Joe was working for had a big store and had everything in it. He would let any Negro get the food and clothes that he would ask him for, and all the Negroes called him a good white man. When there was a big flood or a drought he would fill up sacks of food and clothes, giving them to old Joe and telling him to put everything in the Negroes' houses when he catched them gone. And old Joe did it.

My Uncle said that that went on for about twenty years and that none of the white people or the Negroes knew who Joe Turner was.

The old white man died and all the Negroes went to see him. Old Joe was sitting there, moaning and crying, and all the Negroes was wondering why old Joe was crying. They thought that he should be glad because the old slave owner was dead and gone. So my Uncle said that he went to old Joe and asked him 'Why's you crying, Joe?' and old Joe said:

'You don't know, Jerry, and if you did you would be crying too.'

'No I don't know why,' my Uncle said. 'He was just an old slave owner and no slave owner likes Negroes but only for their work and for what they can get out of them. And you know he didn't like Negroes.'

So old Joe cried out:

'No he didn't like Negroes, he just loved them all and he told me, before he died, to keep on being Joe Turner, but I can't.'

'Why? You's Joe, ain't you?'

'Yes,' he said, 'but without him I'm just old Joe, not Joe Turner.'

'How could he keep you being Joe Turner?' my Uncle asked.

'Call all the Negroes over here. I've got something to tell everybody.'

My Uncle called all the Negroes and old Joe started to tell the story of Joe Turner. He said:

'Do you-all remember when the droughts killed your crop, you-all got food, did you?'

They all said yes.

'And when that big storm blew down you-all's houses and barns, you-all got another house and barn with food for you-all and hay for you-all's mules, did you?'

All the Negroes said, 'Yes, Joe, but who did it?'

'Wait just a minute, I will come to that part. Do you-all remember in 1892 when the big flood took everything and drove you-all out of the bottom on to the hill, and some of you-all people lost their lives, and when the water went down, fourteen days later, old Joe came to the hill and told you-all that you can go home now that the water is gone down? And you did eat while you was in the hill, did you, and when you-all got back home you found beds and flour and meat, molasses, coffee, sugar, oil for your lamps and clothes and new shoes, did you?'

All the Negroes said: 'Yes, but who did it? Come on and tell us, Joe.'

Old Joe shook his head and tears rolled down his cheeks and he said:

'You-all don't know. . . .'

He pointed to the grave where they had buried this old white man and he said:

'You-all Negroes listen to me. That man you-all just seen them white people put six feet in the cold, cold ground, he was your Joe Turner.'

All the Negroes: 'How d'you know, Joe?'

'When you-all would be hunting or fishing, he would fill sacks full of food and clothes and give them to me to put in you-all's houses, and when you-all lost everything me and him stayed up day and night to put beds and food and clothes and everything in your houses. . . . So there is your Joe Turner you've been singing about and crying and dancing and praying to, and he's gone and will never return, and I don't know what you-all Negroes gonna do because there's nobody to love you-all Negroes no more. So goodbye,' said old Joe.

He walked away and my Uncle said that old Joe was never seen any more. Nobody knows what became of old Joe Turner. That was his real name, because his name was Joe and his owner's name was Master Turner.

So that's why I wrote the *Blues* in 1890 and sang about these two great men, a white man and a black one. They both did a good thing before they died. And there's some more Joe Turners in Mississippi yet, and that's the truth about the blues.

PLOUGH-HAND BLUES

Plough-hand has been my name, Lord, for forty years or more
Plough-hand has been my name, Lord, for forty years or more
Yes, I declare I did all I could, Oooo Lord, trying to take care
of my so and so

I ain't gonna raise no more cotton, Lord, and I declare I ain't
gonna try to raise no corn
I ain't gonna raise no more cotton, Lord, and I declare I ain't
gonna try to raise no corn
Now if a mule starts running away with the world, Oooo Lord,
I declare I'm gonna let him go right home.

I wouldn't tell a mule to get up, Lord, if he'd sit down in my lap
I wouldn't tell a mule to get up, Lord, if he'd sit down in my lap
Lord I declare I'm through with ploughing, Oooo Lord, that's
what killed my old grand'pap

Every night I'm hollering, oh gee, getting up in my sleep
Every night I'm hollering, oh gee, getting up in my sleep
Lord I'm always setting my back by and back, Oooo Lord, to
keep my little plough from going too deep.

Vocalion 05452, *Conqueror* 9378. Another version, *Melodisc* 1203.
Verve MG-V-3000-5, Vol. 2

I was a plough-hand for forty years or more.

I remember that I started ploughing in 1900 and the first ploughing that I ever done was with Flat Harry, with two mules pulling it across ploughed ground to even it off for planting chick corn. I ploughed that Harry so well that my father told me that when the corn would be high enough he would let me plough with Prairie Harry, and he did so. I ploughed so good with the Prairie Harry that he told me:

'As soon as the corn and cotton get big enough, I'll let you dirt the cotton with a single shulver.'

And so he did and I've done it so well that he said to me:
'My son, you can handle three ploughs this year; maybe next year you can learn to handle all the ploughs.'

The next year, in breaking-up time, he gave me a turning plough and when I got through listing all the land he gave me a middle-buster, the hardest plough to handle on a farm. I couldn't handle it during the first four or five years. It would throw me down all the time. I knew that all the girls liked a big boy who could handle a middle-buster, so every year I tried to handle it and when I got fifteen years old I could handle all the ploughs on a farm. I was five feet seven inches tall and every Saturday when we would go to meet the train the girls would ask my father: 'Can Bill handle a middle-buster yet?'

And my father would answer: 'Yes, he's my best plough-hand out of my seven boys.'

There was three girls named Mary that would grab me and kiss me. Mary Battle, Mary Mase and the one I liked because she was light skinned and had long sandy hair. The other two Marys was black like me but was built up OK. But they was just black and Mary Crow had light skin and I was crazy about her.

So when I got twenty years old I asked my father to let me marry her. My father said: 'Do you know what you's saying?'

I said: 'Yessir.'

'Oh no you don't. That woman is twenty-eight years old and you's just twenty. My son, you can't do nothing with her, she knows too much and she lives in a red-light house in town.'

'Yessir,' I said, 'I know that because I stayed there one night with her.'

'What?' my father asked. 'Do you know that woman sells her body?'

'Yessir, I bought some of it two times.'

'What?' he repeated. 'What? . . . and where did you get the money?'

'Mother gave me three dollars and told me to go to town and buy me something, anything I wanted, because I was the best plough-hand she had.'

'How long have you been doing this?'

'Just two times, two Saturdays straight.'

So he said:

'You don't know that woman.'

'Oh, yessir, I do. Her name is Mary Crow and she's bright and got big legs.'

'Is that all you know about that woman,' he asked, 'and you want to get married to her?'

'Nossir,' I said. 'She's sweet, she's got nice loving ways and sure can. . . .'

'Shut up before I smack you down,' he said. 'As hard as I tried to make a man out of you I would rather see you dead than to see you married to a red-light district woman. So just get that out of your mind. You can marry Gertrude and not before next year when you'll be twenty-one, in June.'

So the next year, November 11, 1914, me and Gertrude got married and my father was happy.

Every Saturday I would go to town to try to get to see Mary Crow, so one Saturday I went to town before my father did. I found Mary and we went in the room. I heard my father asking after Mary Crow.

'She's got company,' the lady at the door told him.

'What do you mean got company?'

'First come, first served,' she said.

'Who's the man in there with her?' he asked.

'One of the best plough-hands on your farm,' the door lady said.

So my father knew that it was his son Big Bill the plough-hand who sang the blues.

Later on I went to the army and I did not like to plough when I came back, so I wrote the plough-hand blues from being called plough-hand all my young life.

*

I was a plough-hand on a plantation, ploughing corn and cotton. I worked from sun-up to sun-down. They hired another man to help me to plough. So he asked me:

'At what time do we start, and when do we stop?'

'We start when the sun comes up,' I explained, 'and stop when the sun goes down.'

One day the sun was almost out of sight and at the same time the moon was rising.

'Your boss is too smart for me,' the man told me.

'What do you mean, my boss is too smart?'

'Look,' he said, 'your boss takes one sun down and hangs out another one.'

So he left his mule and plough standing in the field and has never been seen since by no one on that plantation.

PARTNERSHIP WOMAN

I got a partnership woman
People, you ought to know how I feel
I'm gonna tell you people
My partner gave me a dirty deal

I took him in my home
Thought it would be fair and square
My woman put me out
And my partner's still livin' there

But if I ever get lucky
And get married again
I'm goin' to buy me a bull dog
Because a dog is a man's best friend

Don't you never think your woman just belongs to you
I declare if she's sweet to you
She'll be sweet to your partner too.

Columbia 30143.

I wrote a song titled *Partnership Woman* and recorded it in 1945 with Big Maceo on piano, Buster Bennett on sax and Little T on drums. It sold very good.

It was a true story, too, because I had a partner, and that's how we call a man when he and another one love each other and that he would give him his clothes and his money and food. We call that a partner. I was raised with this man. I had known him all my life.

His name was Cicero Murphy and when we got to be men he moved to a little town and I still was a plough-hand on a farm—what they call a day-hand. They named you by how you got paid: if you got paid by the month, you was a month-hand, if you got paid by the week you was a week-hand, and if you got paid by the year you was a year-hand.

So I was a day-hand and Cicero was a section-hand. He worked for the Cotton Belt Railroad Company. He changed tires on the railroad, cut the grass and kept the railroad clean and in good shape. They called his job serving track and a section-hand, and he got paid every two weeks.

I went to talk with this little woman, that we called Betty and she told me that she had no man. We got together and I was giving her money every week. Every two weeks she told me she had to go and see her cousin and aunt and they lived in the same town where Cicero worked at. And every two weeks she would go to town, on my money, of course, and stay for three or four days, and she would come back to the plough-hand and stay until the railroad paid off again. She would then kiss me and say:

'Bill, I want to go to town and see my cousin.'

'Yes, Betty,' I'd say, 'here's some money and tell them hello for me.'

She would just take the money and say:

'I'll be gone when you come back tonight, Bill.'

On the fourth day of July there was a big picnic that lasted for four days and nights. Me and Cicero belonged to one of the ball teams and he was off for four days and I was too, so we could be at the picnic to play baseball. He was the pitcher and I was the catcher, and we had to be there on that morning.

I called Betty and asked her:

'Is you going to the picnic?'

'Who's gonna pitch today in the first game?'

'My partner Cicero and I do want you to see him pitch. I know you've never seen him, is you?'

'No, I've never seen him and I don't want to see him pitch no ball.'

'But he's my partner,' I told her, 'and if you like me you'll go with me to see him, because everybody will be there, my people and yours, too.'

'Well, you go now,' she said, 'and I'll be there later on.'

I met Cicero at one of the stands on the picnic ground. We had some drinks and ate some barbecue then sat down on a log and started to talk about our girl friend. I told him my girl's name was Betty.

'Mine's Betty, too,' he said.

'Where does yours live?' I asked.

'In town with her aunt and cousin,' he said. 'I just get a chance to see her every two weeks.'

'I see mine every day,' said I, 'but every two weeks she goes to town to visit her aunt and cousin, and she stays away for three or four days.'

'OK, I see. . . .'

'Betty is light-skinned,' I said. 'She's got long hair and is about five feet tall.'

'Yeah, sure enough. . . .'

We waited and waited. No Betty. So the baseball game was called and we had to go to play. At the end of the ball game, that we winned, me and Cicero look up in a tree and there was Betty. I called her but she wouldn't come and Cicero said to me:

'Don't call her, I see her and I already know her as well as you do, my partner. I am the auntie and cousin she stays in town with every two weeks.'

So I went home with my head hung down, and there she was, looking as pretty as ever.

'Why didn't you tell me you knew Cicero?' I asked her.

'But, Bill, it's you I love, not Cicero. I stay with you more than I do with him.'

She kissed me and pulled her little arms around my neck.

'OK, Betty, you love me.'

So Cicero had dinner with us. We didn't talk about what Betty had done but about the ball game. I had to play for the white people to dance that afternoon, and he stayed at my house for the four days.

I never did forget Cicero and Betty and that's how I wrote that blues, *Partnership Woman*, because any time two men had the same woman and they was partners, she was called a partnership woman.

Yes, that's how I thought up this song, by Betty making me and Cicero get along together, sleep with the same woman and eat together.

After the picnic was over, Cicero went back to town and Betty would say to me:

'Can I go to see Cicero?'

'Yes,' I'd say, 'but don't stay too long. . . .'

And that's, I'm telling you, the real truth about the blues.

HOUSE RENT STOMP

I wrote a guitar solo titled *House Rent Stomp*. No words, just picking the old six-string guitar. That's what I call picking a guitar and making sounds on the six strings, picking them and pushing them up and down, and making the first two strings—E and B—cry, the G   d D talk and the A and E moan, and sliding up and down the neck of the guitar.

Back in 1910 the people didn't dance, they just jumped up and down and stomped the floor, and we guitar pickers we learned to play the guitar that way. We knew but two or three songs to sing, so to play and sing all night would get us tired.

If we played and sang long enough to get them dancing then we would stop singing and just hit on the strings and say to them: 'Rock, children, rock', and they would rock all night long. That's how I learned to play a guitar and not sing, and I got so that I could play four or five different styles without singing.

In 1920, I came to Chicago and the people there asked me to come to their house. Some of them had known me at home and they knew I could play and sing the blues. So I went to their houses and they had fried chicken and pig feet and chittlins for seventy-five cents a plate, and if you could play and sing you got all the eats and drinks free. So I went every Saturday night, and I named one of my guitar solos the *Saturday Night Rub*. I named it like that because that's all they was doing while I was playing. A man and a woman would join up out on the floor and rub their bellies together and stomp and say to me: 'Play the thing, old boy.'

All of them was from some part of the South and had come to Chicago to better their living. Of course I did too, but I would go back every time I got enough money to get a ticket. And those people started to give parties and some

Saturday nights they would make enough money to pay the rent, and so they started to call them 'house rent parties', because they sold chicken, pig feet, home brew, chittlins, moonshine whisky. The musicians didn't have to buy nothing and would get a chance to meet some nice looking women and girls, too.

Me and Louie and Sleepy John Estes and Shorty Jackson and others we played every night for house rent parties, so in 1924 I met Lemon Jefferson, Blind Blake, Lonnie Johnson, Shorty George, Jim Jackson and Barbecue Bob. They all had recorded already and they talked me into trying it. I did in 1925 and I recorded the song *House Rent Stomp* and *Big Bill Blues* on August 14, 1925. But I had recorded three other songs before that, in 1924—*Gonna Tear It Down*, *Tod Pail Blues* and *Dying Day Blues*.

They was never released by me, but by other artists later on, and I didn't get no money out of them.

WHEN WILL I GET TO BE CALLED A MAN?

When I was born in this world, this is what happened to me:
I was never called a man and now I'm fifty-three

I wonder when will I be called a man
Or do I have to wait 'till I get ninety-three?

When Uncle Sam called me I knew I would be called the real
* McCoy*
But when I got in the army they called me soldier boy

I wonder when will I be called a man
Or do I have to wait 'till I get ninety-three?

When I got back from overseas, that night we had a ball
I met the boss the next day, he told me 'Boy get you some
* overall'*

I wonder when will I be called a man
Or do I have to wait 'till I get ninety-three?

I worked on a levee camp and a chain gang too
A black man is a boy to a white, don't care what he can do

I wonder when will I be called a man
Or do I have to wait 'till I get ninety-three?

They said I was undereducated, my clothes was dirty and torn
Now I got a little education, but I'm a boy right on

I wonder when will I be called a man
Or do I have to wait 'till I get ninety-three?

Folkways FA2326

The idea of that song I wrote in 1928, *When Will I Get To Be Called A Man:*

MY SONGS

There was a man that I knew, when I was ten years old, that the white people called a boy. He was about thirty then.

When I went to the army and came back in 1919, well he was an old man then and the white people was calling him Uncle Mackray. So he never got to be called a man, from 'boy' to 'Uncle Mackray'.

And so it is still today. They call all Negro men 'boys' and some of them is old enough to be their father. In fact I do think that some old men is glad to be called boys, but they call you so until you get to be fifty, and at the time you would appreciate to be called a boy they start to call you 'uncle'.

That's the time when I would like to be called a boy, when I get to be fifty or older. It's all right for my sister's kids to call me 'uncle', but not by a man or a woman eighty years old.

WALKING DOWN THE LONESOME ROAD

Have you ever been walking walking down a lonesome road
And did have no place to go and no place to room and board?

Things look so dark, baby, down that road ahead
You get to thinking about the way you's living
And about what your mother said

Things are so lonesome when you haven't got a shelter over
your head
When you could have been at home
Sleeping in a feather bed

This is a lonesome road when you've got to travel all alone
When all you've got in this world is dead and gone.

Recorded in Paris for *Vogue,* September 1951, and in Chicago for *Mercury*
November, 1951.

I had to leave a place once because I had a girl. Her name was Nattie. My boss told me one day that Nattie was too goodlooking for a levee campworker, and I would have to leave. . . .

'And you can't take her with you, and you've got two more days to stay here.'

I went and told Nattie about it. She announced that she would go anywhere I'd go. I told her I would have to leave her or lose my life. So she cried and said:

'I will find you if it's the last thing I do. I will stay until I know where you is, and they can't keep me here, because I love you and not him. But I'll do as I'm told to save your life. So don't worry, I'll play along and some day we'll meet again.'

But I have never seen Nattie again, because she got shot —so I was told by a good friend.

SATURDAY EVENING BLUES

Late one Saturday evening, after the sun went down
It was late one Saturday evening, Lord, after the sun went down
Yes, I went looking for my baby, but she wasn't nowhere around

The wind started hollering, and the rain began to fall
Wind started hollering, I declare the rain began to fall
Yes, if my baby had known how much I loved her, I declare
she'd never would have left me at all

Her picture is still on my dresser, and her gown is still on my
bed
Yes, her picture's on my dresser, I declare her gown is still
hanging on my bed
I'm just sitting here wondering if my baby's still living, Lord,
or is my baby dead

Every Saturday evening, I get as blue as blue can be
Every Saturday evening, I get as blue as blue can be
Yes, we three were so happy, my wife, my guitar and me.

Columbia 37314, *Folkways* FA2326, *Verve* MG V-3000-5, Vol. 1

I was working on a levee camp and I could just come to town
once a week.

My girl lived in town and when I would come I'd stay with
her until two o'clock at night on Sunday and I would leave
so that I could be back to the camp before daybreak, so I
could catch my mules and get out on the levee.

One Saturday I came to town and my girl couldn't be
found, but her picture and her gown was still in the room.

She had left with another man. There was a new mule
track in front of her door and the neighbour had seen her
leaving with another man on a mule. . . .

And we three were happy every Saturday evening because
I would play and sing to her.

OLD MAN BLUES

I wrote a blues titled *Old Man Blues*, recorded with six pieces in 1947.[1] It sold very good. All old men liked it because they knew it was the truth, and it was, too, and a lot of young women shouted when I would sing the verse:

Would you rather be an old man's sweetheart than to be a
*   young man's slave*
An old man carries folding money and will give you what you
*   crave.*

And this is another one that the girls like:
A young man carries a nickel and a nail but an old man carries
*   his dinner pail*
And if an old man promises you something you know he'll
*   never fail.*

'Nickel and nail' means that a young man loves to hear his money rattle. A nickel is a five-cent piece in US money and a nail is made out of steel and made for to build a house and many other things and when they's together in your pocket they'll make a rattling noise.

The young men is not capable of giving women their money and most of them never had any. The women like to go dancing or to be seen with a young man but when it comes to paying board bill and room rent and buying fur coats and dresses and them high-heel shoes they would get an old man because his money don't rattle, his money folds and what you call folding money in the USA is five-, ten-, twenty-, fifty- and one hundred-dollar bills, and all old men carry that kind of money and can get or has got a good job some place and a lot of security on his job—that means he's been working for one company for thirty years and if a job starts laying off men the young ones is laid off first and the

[1] *Columbia* 37502.

old men still get their folding money every pay day and a young woman can pull his whiskers and tickle his chin and call him daddy and put her hand in his pocket and get ten or twenty dollars and he'll say nothing, but a young man will raise hell and call the police.

And about 'would you rather be an old man's sweetheart than be a young man's slave?'

'Be a slave for a young man', as women call it, it is if she's married to a young man and he's got to go to work and be on the job at seven in the morning, his wife has to get up every morning at half-past five to fix his breakfast and his lunch at the same time and when he comes home at six p.m. she must have his meal on the table by the time he washes up and gets ready to eat and while he's eating she must find him a clean shirt and socks and lay them out for him because he's going out with the boys and if he's got a car she don't get to ride in it only on Sundays or when some of their friends die and his car is in the funeral, and as soon as they get back home she has to get out and start getting his meal ready and get his work clothes ready for him the next day to go to work, and when he comes from work if there's any kissing she has to kiss him and bring him his house shoes and the newspaper.

But it's a lot different when a woman is an old man's sweetheart. If she's an old man's wife and he's got to go or be at work at seven o'clock a.m. all she's got to do is to say:

'I don't feel good this morning, honey.'

He'll say:

'All right, baby, just stay in bed, I'll fix breakfast.'

And he fixes his and hers and carries hers to the bed and reads the morning paper to her.

'Darling, should I go tell the doctor to stop by and look at you or should I tell Mother Brown to come and stay with you until I get off from work? If she can't come her son can stay with you until I get off from work. He's nineteen years old and he can give you water and go to the store and get what you want, because I want you to stay in bed and rest.'

And when he comes home from work at six p.m. he picks her up and kisses her.

'How's my little sweetheart today? I brought you something, honey.'

It's a big box of candy, of course.

'And how did Mrs Brown's son treat you today?'

'He was wonderful. He gave me water and food and everything I wanted. He even went and got me some ice cream.'

'I told you sweetheart that boy was a good boy. He's gonna be a good man some day.'

'I think he is now,' she'll say, 'because he's so wonderful and can do most anything. I tried him on cooking and washing dishes and sweeping and mopping and driving the car and a lot of other things and he did a real good job.'

So when the old man gets up next morning she'll say:

'Darling, I want the car. Me and Mr Brown is going fishing today.'

'Who's gonna drive?'

'Mrs Brown's son.'

'Sweetheart, why don't you get him to learn you how to drive?'

So she learns to drive the car and he has some keys made for her and when he comes home from work she hasn't come home yet so he fixes his own meal and when she comes in he kisses her and puts her legs up in his lap and pulls off her shoes and puts her house shoes on and brings her a glass of iced tea, nothing with alcohol in it because she's had plenty of that and when he gives her the iced tea he'll say:

'Sweetheart, ain't you hungry?'

'A little,' she says, 'not much.'

So he'll get the ham that he baked for himself and makes

a sandwich for sweetheart and Mrs Brown's son. After they have eaten, the old man will say to the son of Mrs Brown:

'Why don't you stay all night?'

And sweetheart will say:

'Oh yes do, because I want to make an early start to fishing in the morning. The fish bites better early in the morning, don't they, darling?'

He'll just say 'Yes, sweetheart, they do'.

So he gets up the next morning and fixes breakfast for three and carries it in the dining-room and he pours her coffee and she pours the son's coffee and they get up and say:

'God bless the cook.'

He smiles and says:

'OK, sweetheart, you's a good wife.'

'Darling,' she'll say, 'we're going to drive you to work and when I get through fishing I'll call on your job, and if it's time for you to get off I'll drive by and pick you up and take you home.'

'OK, sweetheart.'

She doesn't call and the car ain't parked in the parking lot when he gets off from work so he gets a street car or a bus and goes home.

She's in his bed and the son of Mrs Brown is in his wife's bed, so he makes tea and gets more sandwiches for three and he goes to bed.

Mrs Brown's son and his wife get up and say:

'Do you want some barbecue?'

'Yes,' he says.

'OK, we'll bring you some because where we go there is the best in town.' And she'll say: 'Don't you go to sleep before I get back.'

And she knows he can't sleep for thinking because Mrs Brown's son is nineteen years old and he is fifty-five and hasn't done nothing but kiss his wife for more than two months . . . so when she's out with Mrs Brown's son he's wondering what's happening, does she just like his company or what does she like about the son of Mrs Brown . . . he's tall and handsome and has curly hair. . . .

So the old man starts checking. And it was just like his friend said: if he wanted to know anything about his wife he would find out himself. And so he did one day: he came back from work too early. The part where he worked broke down and the boss told him they would have it fixed by noon. So he went home and his wife and the son of Mrs Brown was in bed together. . . .

That's what you call 'to be an old man's sweetheart and not a young man's slave'. And that's the truth, too, because that old man was William Lee Conley Broonzy, better known as 'Big Bill'.

LOOKING UP AT DOWN

I'm just like an old rooster
Lord, way out here on a hill
I'm just like an old rooster
Oooh, Lord, way out here on a hill
People, I'm just scratchin'
Oooh, Lord, Big Bill is just trying to live

I'm just like Job's turkey
I can't do nothing but gobble
I'm so poor, baby
I have to lean up against a fence to gabble
Yeah now, baby
Gal, I believe I'll change town
Lord, I'm down so low, baby
Oooh, Lord, gal, I declare I'm looking up at down

The men in the mine, baby
They all looking down on me
Gal, I'm down so low, baby
I'm low as I can be
Yeah now, baby, I'm down as I can be
Yeah, I'm down so low, baby
Oooh, Lord, everybody's looking down on poor me

Everything I get a-hold of, baby
It goes away like snow in June
If I get a chance now, baby, again
I'm going up to the moon
Yeah now, baby,
Gal, I believe I'll change town
Yeah, poor me's down so low, baby
Oooh, Lord, gal, Big Bill is lookin' up at down.

Okeh 05698, *Conqueror* 9761, *French Columbia* BF384.

I remember one time in 1916, in February, I started to plough my farm and get ready to plant cotton and corn. In March I planted my corn, in April I planted my cotton, potatoes, cabbages, onions, turnips, peas, watermelons and a lot of other things. I had two hundred young chickens, twenty-five young pigs, twelve young calves and two young mules. There was fifty acres of cotton, twenty-five acres of corn and twenty acres of peas.

I had borrowed five hundred dollars on my crop to run me and my family and I had bought food for my mules, cows, hogs and I had it in my barn.

Everything I had planted had come up and was growing fine. Then it didn't rain from May 1 until the last of August —we call that a drought—and everything I had planted died, all my chicks had the limber neck and they died too, my hogs had the pink eye and they all died, my cows had the hollow horn and most of them died, too. I lost three mules because the water on my place dried up and it got so hot that my barn caught fire and burned down. All the grass and weeds all over burned up, too. So there was no place to put what mules and cows I had left so that they could find grass or water. The only thing I could do was to walk about five miles and cut prairie grass and bring it back to my mules and cows and then go and work in the mines digging coal.

Two of us brothers went to the mines in Arkansas and two went to the coal mines in Tennessee and got jobs ·there because the man my father got the five hundred dollars from wanted his money or he was going to take our farm and everything on it. So us four brothers had to work for one dollar a day, two meals a day and a bunk to sleep on at night.

So we worked and the white man came and got the one dollar we got for working, and the meals was just dinner and supper. Many days I worked from five o'clock a.m. till twelve noon before I got anything to eat and I wore the same shoes, overall and underwear from June until November and many nights I did not pull my clothes off. I slept with them on and every morning the bell rang for us to get up and go into the mines.

There was fifty men in the mine where I was working. There was a place they called the pit and the boss put me down in the pit. It was twenty feet deeper than the real mine, so all the other miners was looking down on me and that's one of the verses in *Looking Up At Down*.

I didn't have a penny in my pocket and was tired and weak and just could talk and I had lost weight and that's what I mean about being as poor as Job's turkey and he was so poor that he had to lean up against a fence to gobble.

Well when the boss would say it's time to go and eat or go to sleep, many evenings I would sit down and lean up against a pile of coal or anything to rest, so I would be able to walk to the place to eat and sleep.

Every meal we had beans and salt meat for five months. After one month I got tired of beans and had to eat them anyway. That's how I got used to eating beans, fat meat and corn bread.

The little house where we ate and slept was out on the hill. That's how I got the first verse to *Looking Up At Down*, because lots of times when it was time to eat you would have to scratch and fight to get to the table to get something to eat, so I was just scratching and fighting and poor Bill was trying to live.

This song was recorded in 1939 with Josh Altheimer on piano and Fred Williams on drums.

BLACK, BROWN AND WHITE

This little song that I'm singing about
People you know is true
If you're black and got to work for a living
This is what they will say to you

They say if you's white, you's all right
If you's brown, stick around
But as you're black
Mmm, Mmm, Brother, git back, git back, git back

I was in a place one night
They was all having fun
They was all buying beer and wine
But they would not sell me none

They said if you's white, 'll be all right
If you's brown, stick around
But if you're black
Mmm, Mmm, Brother, git back, git back, git back

Me and a man was working side by side
This is what it meant
They was paying him a dollar an hour
And they was paying me fifty cents

They said if you's white, should be all right
If you's brown, you could stick around
But as you're black
Mmm, Mmm, Brother, git back, git back, git back

I went to an employment office
Got a number and I got in line
They called everybody's number
But they never did call mine

They say if you's white, should be all right
If you's brown, stick around
But as you're black
Mmm, Mmm, Brother, git back, git back, git back

I helped win sweet victory
With my little plough and hoe
Now I want you to tell me, brother
What you gonna do 'bout the old Jim Crow

Now if you's white, you's all right
If you's brown, stick around
But if you's black
Oh, Brother, git back, git back, git back

(This is a verse that has not been recorded. Big Bill often adds it to his song.)

I helped build the country
And I fought for it too
Now I guess you can see
What a black man has to do.

Vogue 134, *Emarcy-Mercury* MG36137, *Folkways* FG3586

I wrote a song in 1945 titled *Black, Brown And White.* I tried RCA Victor, Columbia, Decca and a lot of little companies, but none of them would record it. They wanted to hear it, and after I had played and sung it they would refuse.

'And why do you want to record such a song?' they would ask. 'Nobody would buy it.'

'What's wrong with it? I would like to know. What I say is just about the way the working Negro is treated in this country on all jobs in the South, in the North, in the East and in the West, and you all know it's true.'

'Yes,' they would say to me, 'and that is what's wrong

with that song. You see, Bill, when you write a song and want to record it with any company, it must keep the people guessing what the song means. Don't you say what it means when you're singing. And that song comes right to the point and the public won't like that.'

I kept on trying it anyway. When I came to France in 1951 I told Mr Hugues Panassié about it. He asked me why and I played it to him. He said:

'Yes, I like it. Do you want to record it?'

'Well I've been trying for six years but no company would record it for me.'

'Before you leave France it will be recorded,' he said.

And so it was, on September 21 of that same year, and released soon after. I carried a copy back with me to the States and I played it to them. 'We like the music,' they said, 'but not the words.'

One day I got a letter from the Mercury Recording Company that told me to get ready with about eight songs for a recording session. That was in January 1952. I recorded *Black, Brown And White* that time, but it hasn't been released.* Of course I know that the Mercury Company recorded it because of Mr John Hammond. I played it to him once in 1946. Him and Alan Lomax both liked it. Mr Hammond said to me:

'Bill, that's a good song you've got there, why don't you record it?'

'I've tried nearly all the companies, but they don't like it.'

He smiled and said: 'They will.' So that's why it has been finally recorded in the States, too.

Of course there's nothing wrong with the song but the Negroes don't like it because it says: *If you's black, git back.* And I don't blame them because we all Negroes in the USA have been getting back all of our lives and we's tired of getting back. But this song doesn't mean for a Negro to get

* Note: Two versions have since been issued, as mentioned after the lyrics.

back, it just tells what has happened on jobs where Negroes go.

*

I remember once I went to an employment office and everybody had to get a number and get in line. Then you had to wait until your number was called. I stayed in line for about five hours. There was about fifty of us in this line and only two Negroes, me and a Negro woman.

After they had called the white men and women, one of the managers came out and said to me and the Negro woman:

'Sorry but we don't hire any Negroes today and don't know when we will.'

So this woman walked away and I said to her:

'Let's catch the street car.'

'I ain't got street car fare,' she told me, 'I've spent my last seven cents to come out here. I was so sure of getting a job because the ad in the newspaper said they wanted fifty women and I did see but about fifteen women there. So I stayed in line.'

'You's a Negro,' I said to her.

'The paper just said women.'

'You's a Negro,' I said again.

'But I'm a woman, and I know it because I've got five children and my husband got gassed in 1918 in the army.'

'You's still a Negro, and I am too, so we have to get back, can't you see what I mean?'

'I knew about it in the South, but not in the North.'

'And where are you now?'

'I'm in Chicago.'

'It's the same in New York,' I told her. 'All over the USA it's the same soup, but it's just served in a different way.'

*

That song doesn't tell the Negro to get back but just about

where and who tells them to get back all the time, and reminding the one who says it.

I, Big Bill, don't like to get back, I'm a blues singer and I sing about it.

*

One of the verses I sing is about me and a man working together—a white man of course.

I was working in a foundry. I was a moulder there for seven years and I showed all the other moulders there how to put up a mould, how to cut their sand and how to put a pattern in the mould, because I was an all around man. When the boss would get a new pattern he would always call me and I would make anything he gave me.

So one day he called me in the office and said: 'Bill, take this man and show him how to make a mould.'

So I learned him how to make moulds and we worked together for a year. One day he asked me where I was living and he came home with me. We had been stopping and getting drinks together every pay day so far, but that day we bought a bottle of whisky and went to my house. We had a meal together and then started drinking. He got drunk and started to call me a fool.

'What do you mean, I'm a fool?'

'Just this,' he said, and he laid the stub from his cheque on the table. 'That's what I mean, my friend, let me see yours.'

So I laid mine on the table.

'Your cheque is of fifty dollars and mine is for a hundred. Can't you see you's a fool? You's my boss and have learned me everything I know and I get twice as much as you do. You's been working here for seven years and haven't got a raise.'

'Yes I have, when I started here seven years ago I was getting twenty-five dollars a week.'

He laughed and said:

'When I started one year ago I was getting fifty-five dollars a week and now after you learned me to mould I get a hundred dollars a week. Don't you see you's a fool. You know more about moulding than the man who owns the place.'

Of course he was Polish and hadn't been in the US for long. The next year he was my boss, and when he started to lay off, all the Negroes were laid off first.

So you can see what I mean by *if you's black git back*. And it happens in other parts of the world too, just in a little different way.

*

Once I went in a bar where they was selling whisky, beer, wine and other kinds of drinks. I was with three white men. One of them ordered four shots of whisky and we all drank. The bartender took my glass and broke it after I had drunk. Every time I had killed a drink he would break the glass I had used.

The men I was with said:

'Let's make him break some more glasses.'

So they kept on ordering and he kept on breaking glasses. Then one of the men with me said:

'Bill, let's drink some champagne, those glasses are expensive, let's see will he break them, too.'

So they ordered champagne, I drank and he broke three of them glasses.

Finally the boss walked in and he got mad:

'Stop breaking them glasses.'

The bartender answered:

'You told me every time a Negro drinks out of a glass to break it. That's what I did.'

Everybody in the place laughed and he wouldn't sell me
no more whisky. So we left and the glasses cost more than
the drinks we had in there.

*

I do think that the reason why the Negroes don't like the
song *Black, Brown And White* is because they don't want to
be a Negro and they try not to look like one. They fix their
hair, wear their clothes, talk and act like the American white
man.

The white man has a million dollars and I just have seven
thousand dollars in the bank and a job paying sixty dollars
a week. I'll pay six thousand dollars for a Cadillac, a hundred
and ten dollars for a suit, forty-five dollars for a hat, forty
dollars for my shoes. I'll spend all the money I have just
trying to dress, ride and look like the white man. I'll get the
brightest Negro woman I can so she'll look white. I'll
straighten my hair and try to go in places where I'm not
wanted. They tell me:

'We don't serve Negroes in here.'

I get mad because I think I look like a white man with
my hair straightened, that hundred-and-ten-dollar suit, my
Cadillac and a yellow woman who's hair is just as straight
as a white one's.

So why don't they want me in here? I have American
money and I pay tax. Is it because I'm black? Oh well,
remember that song that Louis Armstrong sings called
Black And Blue:

I can't hide what's on my face.

In every place I go, all the people I meet of different races
is glad to say and to be from where they was born. But me,
when anybody asks me if I'm from Mississippi, I'll say yes
but I'm mad and don't like to talk about it, because I was
born poor, had to work and do what the white man told me

to do, a lot of my people were mobbed, lynched and beaten. The ones who owned something, the white man wanted his wife or his best horse, he had to give it up. For everything I raised on my farm, the white man was setting his price; he paid me what he wanted to give and I had to take it. So when I went to the North I tried to be like him and I got me a white woman and a big car. Some time I'd have no money to buy gas but I'd pawn my watch or my ring, so the other Negroes could see Big Bill's car and white woman. I did have the white woman because I wanted her, not to hurt anyone. I just wanted to be and act like a white man. I had a black wife at home, and in the South the white man had a white wife and a Negro woman, children by them both, and in no place he went had he to get back for nobody, and everybody liked him. So that's the reason why I tried to play and do things like him.

Even a half-white Negro was treated better than a black Negro. So I straightened my hair, changed my way of talking and walking, always trying to do things like a white man so I wouldn't have to get back. But since I've been in other parts of the world and seen that I'm not the only black man in the world and that all the other black people in the world like and love each other, it's different.

The American Negroes, they make fun out of each other. If you's from a different State in the USA, if your hair is frizzy and you's real black, all the northern Negroes who have their hair straightened and know the town, instead of trying to show me how to act and do, they'll just laugh and call me a Mississippi Negro and they don't seem to know that if their hair is straight it's just because their mother cheated on their father with a white man who's their real father.

When I came to the North I did not just come there to get a white woman or just to be with one to get back at the

Negro woman, because she could have a white man in Mississippi, and I could walk down the street beside or on the same side of the street as a white woman. But lots of times I would wonder why a white man would kill me if he'd seen me with a white woman. What is it she's got that my Negro woman ain't got? He has a white woman and he has a Negro woman, too. So I came to the North and tried it. I tried everything I had seen him do, then I would go home and look in my looking-glass and I could still see Mississippi, and the next morning when I got up my hair would be gone back home and I'd have to straighten it again. And in a lot of places that I would take that white woman, she would go in there to get food and drinks for me and her because they don't allow Negroes, but I didn't care because I was in a big fine car like a white man, I had a white woman and she could get anything I could pay for. So I was happy. She would come back and say that the bill was ten dollars and it wasn't but three dollars, I would just say:

'OK, darling, let's ride around in the park.'

I tried everything not to be made to get back. I changed everything. I even learned to play my guitar differently and sing different songs. So I found out that a white woman, fine clothes, a big car and straightened hair, a change of walking and talking don't hide what's on your face and so, if you's black in the USA you've got to git back, git back, git back. . . .

White woman, white dog and red car don't help any and I think that loving one another is the best way. Let's try it.

WHEN I'VE BEEN DRINKING

I don't need no money, I got luck oil on my hand
I don't want no woman, boys, always raising sand

When I've been drinking, yes, when I've been drinking
Now when I come home, baby, please let me lay down and rest

I'm looking for a woman, that ain't never been kissed
Maybe we can get along and I won't have to use my fist

When I've been drinking, yeah, when I've been drinking
Now when I come home, baby, please let me lay down and rest

I want a job to go to work at twelve, get off at one
Have an hour for dinner, boys, my day's work'd be done

When I've been drinking, yes, when I've been drinking
Now when I come home, baby, please let me lay down and rest

I want somebody to pet me and feed me in the bed
Talk, baby, talk to me, gal, when you go to comb my head

When I've been drinking, yes, when I've been drinking
Now when I come home, baby, please let me lay down and rest

I want to be taken out of the bed, baby, put in a wheel chair
Roll me anywhere now, baby, Big Bill don't care

Gal, when he's been drinking, yeah, when I been drinking
Now when I come home, baby, please let me lay down and rest.

Okeh 06303, *Conqueror* 9931, *Columbia* 37474 *Columbia* WL111

One day, back in 1900, I heard my uncle sing a song that he called *Keep On Drinking To Drive My Blues Away*.

My mother would get mad at him when she knew that he

had had a drink, and he would sing the song after my mother was out of the house.

My father and my uncle both drinked. They called it 'mountain dew' because they had to go to the mountain to get it. You go to the hill and go down in behind the hill and put your jug and money on a stump, walk away and come back about ten minutes later—your jug was full of mountain dew and your change would be on the stump, too, if there was any.

WPA RAG

In 1934 I wrote a rag titled *WPA Rag*. The first verse was an old levee camp holler:

Oh I feel like hollering but the town is too small.

And the other part is:

When we was gambling shooting dice we would get a point.

When we was rolling dice and when they stopped on six and the other on four, we called that ten for a point and we would roll the dice and say: 'Oh six-four I call you.'

The next verse is:

I want all you women and I mean all you stags to spend your money.

Where I play this *WPA Rag* the stags mean anytime a party was given and there was nothing there but men, they call it a stag-party, and where I would be playing the man who owns the place likes to hear me sing that verse because I tell everybody to spend their money and if they had no money to spend it was time for them to go home.

In that time just about all the men and women was on the WPA. That was the only work you could get at that time and it lasted a long time, too. Louis Armstrong recorded a song called *WPA*, Casey Bill and Peetie Wheatstraw recorded a *WPA Blues*. In that time anything you'd say about WPA was all right because that was all you had to live on.

WPA, PWA, CWA, all of these was work projects for men and women. Me and my manager both was on the WPA together. There was no recording at that time. It was easy for us to get a job on the WPA because we had been in the army in 1918 and they called us old veterans. All old veterans had no trouble getting on the WPA.

I remember one day I was working on the WPA, laying concrete on 47th Street in Chicago. We was eating dinner and one of the boys said:

'Big Bill I heard a record and it sounds just like you and your Memphis Five.'

'Where at?' I asked.

'When we get off from work I'll take you by the place.'

'All right.'

So I went with him and sure enough it was the *WPA Rag*. I had recorded it about five months before 1 had got that job. Of course the WPA had been going on for about a year before I got broke enough to get in there.

We had a boss that we called 'Big George' and when he would see one of the men standing, leaning on his shovel he would holler:

'Get up off that shovel, boy, if you's tired go to the office and check out, and come back tomorrow and try it again.'

So we all started to tease each other about leaning on our shovel and I got to like working on the WPA.

Of course I was used to working anyhow, because I had a job all the time that I was playing music and making records. I worked every day and played music at night, because I didn't make enough money, just playing music and recording, to take care of my family. So it didn't bother me to work.

Two or three of my friends got sick from the heat, but it didn't bother me because it hadn't been so long that I had come from the Mississippi, off a farm, and I had worked in a foundry, carrying hot iron and it wasn't hot at all to me out there.

One day Big George said to me:

'Big Bill, how tall is you?'

'I'm six feet and one and a half inches tall.'

'You's just right for what I want to be done.'

'What is it that you want done, George?'

'I've got to have a hole dug six feet deep and four feet

wide and five feet long and you's just the man for the job
and I know you'll work and do as you's told.'

That made me feel good for the boss to say that in front
of all the other men not knowing that they was going to
have fun out of me.

Of course they all knew I was afraid of snakes, and the next
day at eight a.m. I started digging and I heard them all laughing. At noon I stopped and had dinner. The boss said to me:

'The way you dig, you'll be finished by three o'clock.'

When I was about six feet deep, I felt something on my
back and something around my legs. So I straightened up
and there was five little snakes there about as big as your
finger and about two feet long.

When I came to myself I was at home lying down and
heard my wife say:

'What's the matter and why did you bring that snake
home with you?'

One of the snakes had crawled around in front of me and
I had run so fast that he couldn't fall off my chest.

The next day, I went back to work.

'Why did you go?' asked Big George. 'You left before
time to get off.'

'Oh, did I?'

'You sure did. Was someone sick at your home?'

'Yes.'

'Who?'

'Me.'

'What was wrong with you?'

'I've never seen so many snakes in one hole before. Did
you, George?'

He was so tickled that he just walked away and every
time I would go up to him asking him what to do, he would
laugh and walk off, so when I asked him for the fifth time
he said 'go to the office'.

There the head man looked at me and tears were falling from his eyes and he couldn't hardly talk, but he did manage to tell me to go home and come back tomorrow.

One of the boys had called my wife and told her about what had happened. I thought that the big boss had fired me when he had said 'go home'. When I got there my wife and the kids was laughing about what the boys had told on the phone. So every day for five days I did do nothing but go to work and come back home.

Later I found out that George had the boss to put them snakes in the hole on me and they told me how I got out of that hole and left there running so fast and passed by all of them, humming the blues. I laughed too, when they told me that and when I looked at the hole then I did laugh, because I had filled it back up almost and the tracks I made leaving there was about twelve feet apart.

So that's the truth about the *WPA Rag*.

I also played with Casey Bill on the *WPA Blues* that he recorded. His real name is William Weldon. He was born in Pine Bluff, Arkansas, in 1909, July 10, and he's in California now.

JUST A DREAM

It was a dream, just a dream I had on my mind
It was a dream, just a dream I had on my mind
And when I woke up, baby, not a thing could I find

I dreamed I went out with an angel, and had a good time
I dreamed I was satisfied, and nothing to worry my mind
(I dreamed I was in heaven, sitting down around the throne
I dreamed I had a pretty angel, playing back in my home)
But it was a dream, just a dream I had on my mind
Lord, and when I woke up, baby, not an angel could I find

I dreamed I played policy, and played the horses too
I dreamed I'd winned so much money, I didn't know what
*   to do*
(I dreamed I had a million dollars, had a mermaid for my
*   wife*
I dreamed I'd winned the Brooklyn Bridge, on my knees shoot-
*   ing dice)*
But it was a dream, just a dream I had on my mind
Lord, and when I woke up, baby, not a penny could I find

I dreamed I was married, and started a family
I dreamed I had ten children, and they all looked just like me
But that was a dream, just a dream I had on my mind
Lord, and when I woke up, baby, not a child could I find.
(I dreamed I was in the White House, sitting in the President's
*   chair.*
I dreamed he shaked my hand, said Bill I'm glad you're here,
But that was a dream, just a dream I had on my mind
Lord, and when I woke up, baby, not a chair could I find.)

Big Bill has recorded at least three different versions of this song. The words of the two most famous recordings are given here. With Joshua Altheimer on piano they were made in February 1939 (*Vocalion* 04706, *Columbia* 30153) and September 1939 (*Vocalion* 05259). Shortly before his death, Big Bill recorded this again on *Verve* MGV-3000-5, Vol. 5.

One night there was a girl at a house party where I was playing. At a certain moment I was in the kitchen having a drink of moonshine whisky and I talked to this girl.

'When I get off from playing tonight, I'm gonna take you home with me.'

'Take *who* home?' she asked.

'Yes,' I said, 'I'm gonna take you home with me tonight.'

'That's just a dream you've got on your mind, the girl answered, and you can get it off because my husband is coming after me at twelve o'clock sharp.'

That's how I got the idea to write that song, *Just A Dream.*

KIND-HEARTED WOMAN

I've got a kind-hearted woman
Lord, she's kind to me every day
I've got a kind-hearted woman
Lord knows she's kind to me every day
Lord, she always gives me spending money
Lord knows she always lets me have my way

More women you got
Kind hearted they will be
More women you got
Lord, the kind hearted they will be
Lord, because the one that I've got
Ain't nothing she won't do for me

My woman says she loves me
She will do anything that she can
My woman loves me
She says 'But, Bill, please don't get down wrong'
She says 'If you do
They will get a long telegram down home'

My baby said she'd give me
All the money she wins
My baby told me she would give me
All the money she wins
She said 'Bill, I will buy you a coffin
Boy, and a grave just to put it in.'

Vogue LD 072.

I wrote a song called *Kind-Hearted Woman.* I remember
once I did have a kind-hearted woman, and she really was
kind-hearted too. Gee, and what a woman! She weighed
three hundred and three pounds and was just as wide as

she was tall. She was five feet and seven inches tall and she measured the same from side to side. When she got mad at me I could feel that weight all around the place.

She's kind to me every day
She always gives me spending money
She always lets me have my way . . .

This is what it means: every morning she gets up and leaves me in bed. Before she goes to her job she gives me five dollars and tells me:

'Now, darling, you get me some milk, potatoes and a pair of stockings and have my shoes repaired and you'd better get a chicken for supper, don't forget to pay the light and gas bills, and get me an half pint, too. Now don't you spend all that money, darling, because we's going to go to the show tonight. You can buy you some cigarettes and ride around in the car because I know it has two gallons in it, so you can have your way today, but don't forget to get what I told you to get for me, honey, and be home at five because I'll be back at six and I want you there with a good supper ready, and don't forget my snuff because I'm just about out, I got about three more dips left in my box, and, honey, feed the hogs and goats and cows and take in the clothes I washed last night and put on the line . . . you know I let you have your way.'

More women you got
The kind hearted they will be . . .

That's because that woman I had, she weighed three hundred and three pounds. I remember the first night that I stayed at her house. She says to me 'Get in the bed' and I did get in.

When she got up and pulled off her clothes I got scared and when she sat on the side of the bed I thought I was going out through the ceiling because the side I was on came up so high; I got swimming in the bed and when she got in it the covers never touched me, it was just like sleeping under a small tent.

One night I woke up and I wanted to go to the toilet. She had one of her legs across me and I couldn't move. She was snoring, grunting, wailing, she was doing everything in her sleep. I pinched her and she did not wake up. Then I bit her on her arm and she woke up:

'The mosquitoes sure is bad tonight, aren't they, baby?'

'Sure, baby,' I said and I got loose, went to the toilet and rested.

> *Big Bill don't get down wrong*
> *Because if you do so*
> *Your mother will get a telegram down home . . .*

So I laughed and said:

'What is you talking about and what do you mean?'

'I mean,' she said, 'your mother will get a chance to wear that black dress she got if you intercourse with my money, so just don't do that if you don't want your mother and father to cry because if I find out you's getting down wrong you's a dead duck.'

And that's the last verse:

> *My baby told me she would give me*
> *All the money she wins*
> *And will buy me a coffin and a grave to put it in . . .*

'Get down wrong' means that if you got a woman who's working, or a gambling woman, and she don't want you to do nothing but lay in bed, read and make love to her when she comes home, and she lets you count the money she wins or let you take her cheque, chase it, pay all the bills out of it and bring her the change back, she'll count it and check all the bills you said you paid. If her cheque was fifty dollars, you paid out forty dollars and give her nine dollars change, then you've got down wrong and you's going to be a dead duck, and that means that you'll be just as dead as a baked duck. Because while you was out paying the bills she was trying out her razor and her pocket knife, wondering which one should she kill you with.

I remember once there was a woman, we called her Black Saddy, she was real dangerous with a razor and she always kept it sharp. Her man's name was Abraham and we called him 'One-Eyed Abe'.

Him and Saddy had a fight. Abe beat Saddy and left her lying on the road. We all thought she was dead and we was all sitting at a card table, playing Georgia Skin. One-Eyed Abe was sitting with his back to the door. Saddy came in, put her razor around Abe's neck and pulled it. We could see the blood coming down his shoulder, so we said:

'Abe, Saddy has cut your neck.'

'That woman is afraid of me,' he said. 'See, she's running down the road. As soon as I play this hand out I'm gonna get on my horse and catch her and give her a good beating for putting her hand around my neck while I was gambling. She knows I don't like for nobody to bother me when I'm gambling.'

So one of the boys said:

'But, Abe, you's dead. . . .'

'Oh, man, deal the cards and stop kidding with me. I don't like to be kidded when I'm gambling, so please deal the cards.'

So another boy told him:

'Abe, you's dead, your head is cut off. . . .'

'You's crazy. Don't you hear me still talking?'

The boys all said:

'Yeah sure, we hear you talking but we see your head is cut off, too, and if you don't believe us just shake your head, man, and you'll see what we mean.'

'Is you all crazy? OK, I'll shake my head.'

Abe shook his head and his head fell off on the table. The boys hollered out:

'We told you so!'

And that was the last of old One-Eyed Abe. We buried him the next day in the levee. That was a man who was dead and didn't know it. Of course Saddy knew he was dead because she kept her razor that sharp all the time and she knew that old One-Eyed Abe was a dead duck.

Mrs Saddy was a kind-hearted woman and there was a lot of them in Mississippi. I know it because I had one, too. Her name was Narcice and she cut me down the back. I did not notice it and I sat there for nearly two hours, playing my guitar. When I got ready to go home I got up and my pants fell down because she had cut my belt too and my shoes was full of blood. They took me to a doctor, they sewed my back up and they had to put thirty-two stitches. Yeah, brother, and that's the truth about the blues, too.

I recorded *Kind-Hearted Woman Blues* for the Vogue Recording Company in Paris, France, in 1952, but I've been singing them kind of blues for forty-five years or more.

*

I remember when my baby girl was about seven years old, I had to tell her a story before she would go to sleep at night. Every night, when I would come home she was awake, waiting for me. When she heard me open the door she'd say:

'Is that you, Daddy?'

'Yes, Catherine, this is your Daddy.'

'I'm waiting for my story.'

I had been telling her about Little Red Riding Hood and about the Three Bears for five years now and every time I would tell her a story she would laugh herself to sleep. So I said to myself 'I'm going to tell her one she's never heard before and I know she'll laugh herself to sleep right away.'

So I sit down on the side of her bed and start to tell her

about Abraham and Black Saddy. She stayed right still and it took me about twenty-five minutes to tell her the whole story.

Catherine did not close her eyes during all the time that I was telling her this story. She just looked at me and she didn't smile at all. She just waited until I got through telling her about Abraham and Black Saddy. When I got to the end of it I said:

'Well, Catherine, you ain't laughing. What's wrong to-night, don't you like that story?'

She sat up in the bed:

'Daddy, that's not a story, that's a lie and Mother told me anybody who tells lies the bogey man will get them. I'm afraid for you, Daddy, you'd better sleep with me so I can keep the bogey man off my Daddy tonight, so undress and get over behind me and try to go to sleep, if you can after telling me that.'

*

One other day I was in a barber shop sitting in a barber chair and the barber was cutting my hair. I started telling this story about One-Eyed Abe and Black Saddy. When I got through telling it the barber just grunted. When he got through cutting my hair, I got up from the chair:

'You gave me a good hair cut, how much do I owe you?'

He grunted and said to me:

'For what you just told me you don't owe me nothing. That one haircut is on the house. So goodbye, Big Bill, and don't forget to come back when you've got a bigger lie to tell.'

My Friends

*For this chapter, Mr. Bruynoghe has accumulated additional informa-
tion since the original edition was published. In cases where additional
factual material has become available, it has been added to the text in the
form of footnotes. The existence of additional information is indicated by the
appearance of a letter marking, such as (a). The detailed footnote, under
the appropriate letter, appears on Page 150.*

ONCE I worked for a man who was a talent scout for the RCA-Victor and the Columbia recording companies. One night he called me up and wanted to see me. So I got in my car and went to meet him.

'There are two men in East Saint Louis who both are good blues singers,' he said to me. 'Will you go down there, get them and bring them back to Chicago? I'll give you a hundred dollars, fifty for your spending money and here's a bottle of whisky.'

So I left Chicago the next day and I got into St Louis at about six p.m. I had the two men's addresses and names. They both was called Mike. One was 'Red Mike' and the other was 'Black Mike' and the addresses was not far apart. I stopped in a rib joint, had a good meal and it was about nine o'clock, so I drove down the street, listening for some music. When I heard some I got out, locked my car and walked down the street.

I met a little man and asked him:

'Do you know Red Mike or Black Mike?'

He said no, so I asked him again and he still said no. It came to me that a dollar talks so I put my hand in my pocket, got out two one-dollar bills, handed them to him and said:

'Do you know those two men?'

He looked up at me.

'Yes,' he said, then grinned. 'Come with me.'

We walked about three blocks. The man stopped, looked up at me, grinned again.

'What do you want with these men?' he asked.

I told him it was to make records. Then he smiled again and said:

'I am Black Mike and Red Mike is in that house. I'll go and get him.'

The Mike I had been talking to was a real light-skin Negro. He came back with Red Mike who was as black as a patent leather shoe.

We went across the track and got some moonshine. I told them that we had to be in Chicago tomorrow morning at noon. I bought them a fruit jar of moonshine. They drunk the first one right down, so I had to get another one and each jar held half a gallon. Of course they had a little help, you know, Big Bill was the man who had found the two Mikes and when we three got in Chicago I had a tough time telling the men of the recording company which was which.

They recorded some good blues. Red Mike made *Hell Ain't But A Mile And A Quarter* and Black Mike made *Pussy Foot Baby*.

Of course I got to be their friend and I took them back to St Louis. There I met their mother and father. Their mother was a brown-skin Negro. Red Mike's father was a real black man. Black Mike's father was a white man. So you see what I mean: the two men had the same mother but they had different fathers. But both of them could really sing. They were born in Duck Hill, Mississippi, not far from my home. I also recorded one of Red Mike's songs. This happened in 1937.

We called SLEEPY JOHN ESTES' way of playing and singing the blues 'crying the blues', because he did really cry when he was singing work songs or some blues. His best songs were *Married Life Blues, Good Old Cabbage Green, My Mother Don't Allow Me To Stay Out All Night Long, Don't Take Money From A Poor Boy Like Me*, and many others.

The work songs he was singing was really our daily work songs. I remember sometime when I was working on the railroad. The name was the 'yellow dog' and I was in the gang called the 'lining gang'. There was eight of us and we all had bars. The bars was six and a half feet long. We called them lining bars and John Estes would do the calling for us to line track every morning.

When he would call us to start to work, this was his words:

'*Every morning every motherchild grab a bar and follow me.*'

Most of the time we would have to walk a half mile to where we worked from our gang cars where we eat and sleep at.

John Estes would sing all the way and when we would get to the place where we had to work at, John Estes would holler:

'*Gang around me, boys, like flies around sugar.*'

And we would and then he would yell:

'*All men to their places like horses to their traces.*'

That meant to put your bar under the rail and he would yell out to us:

'*Is every motherchild got a hold? If not get one and a good one.*'

There was a white man about a hundred feet ahead of us showing John Estes which way he wanted the track to move and John Estes would sing it to us and we moved the track.

One day the boss kept on giving signs to us and we all just stood still and didn't move the track. So the boss got mad and walked up to us and said: 'What's the matter with you damn Negroes?' We couldn't say nothing so he looked at John Estes and said to him: 'What's wrong?' John Estes didn't say nothing, then the white man hitted him. John woke up, started to sing and we started to work, too. So after that we all called John Estes the sleeping track caller and that's how he got the name 'Sleepy John Estes'.

He had a woman on the gang, too, and we called her 'Crying Mary' because he beat her almost every day. He had to do it because if he didn't she wouldn't cook or do nothing and after he'd give her a good beating she would cook some of the best pies and biscuits and wouldn't burn the ham. If he didn't beat her, she would burn up everything, even the boss's food.

That's all that John Estes was doing: beat Mary and sing for us to work by. Everything we was doing during the day was by John Estes' singing. If we wanted to go to the toilet during work time we would tell John Estes and he would sing it to the boss. When he would get the sign from the boss he would sign to us:

'*Everybody lay their bar down, it's one to go.*'

Of course there was no toilet, we just stooped behind a bush or a tree, and when the one that went off comes back he would holler:

'*All men to their places like horses to their traces.*'

One day we had stopped to let a train pass. The boss always stopped us from work about ten minutes before the train got to us, so we could get all the bars out the track and he would tell us to stand back from the track. John Estes was asleep and when the train got up to us it blowed. He got scared when he heard it and he ran off. After the train had passed the boss said: 'Where's John Estes at?'

We said we didn't know.

'I'll be damned,' said the boss, 'there's always something wrong with him, if he ain't sleeping he has run off. All you Negroes get out in the woods and don't come back until you find John Estes.'

Of course we was glad because we couldn't work without John Estes. So we went looking for him and found him about three miles away dead asleep. We didn't wake him up. We just sat down on a log under a big tree and went to sleep too.

About three hours later one boy woke up and said: 'We'd better go.' So we woke John Estes up and we went back to where we was working at and on our way we made up a good lie to tell the boss where we had been. John Estes had it fixed for us because the boss didn't think John would lie or would lie to him, and we all knew that. So John said:

'I'll tell him a bear had run me up a tree and you all had to run the bear away before I could come down out the tree.'

So when we all got back to our place to work we saw the boss lying down under a tree and John Estes said:

'That's one lie I won't have to tell old boss because he's asleep now and it's time to go home, so I'll just wake him up.'

So John Estes called the boss. He woke up and said:

'Where have you been?'

'Right here, boss, right here beside you.'

So we put the hand car on the track and all of us went home together. The boss didn't say a word all the way and John Estes started a song and we all joined in and helped him to sing until we got to our gang cars.

After we all had eaten we went out on the grass and laid down. John Estes told the gang about what had happened and we all got a good laugh and went to bed.

John Estes is just about eighty-seven years old now because I was nineteen years old then and all of this happened between 1912 and 1915. I would run off from home just to work under John Estes' singing and he would let me sing with him some time.

In 1922 I met him in Chicago where he was singing the blues. (a)

An artist like BIG MACEO had a way of playing that was just strictly his own. Of course he did one good thing before his death: he started to learn a boy named Johnnie Jones to play just like him, and Johnnie can really play like Big Maceo; if he could sing as good no one could tell the difference.

I remember one day that I went to the train with Big Maceo. He was going to Detroit, Michigan, to visit his sister and brother there. I met three of his sisters, two of his brothers and one of his nieces when I went to visit him in Detriot. He had a very nice family, some of which was church members.

Big Maceo was liked very much by all musicians and blues singers all over the States and he was a good friend of Tampa Red before I knew him. It's at Tampa Red's house that I first met him and when I first heard him play I told everybody that he was a man who really loved the blues and could really play and sing them, too.

When Tampa Red introduced us he started to call me Big Boy and we got to be just as brothers. He was Tampa Red's piano player and they had played a long time together before I knew him. I was then playing in a night club on the West side of Chicago and Joshua Altheimer, my piano player, had died in 1940, so we talked about him playing with me and he said OK.

I went to my boss, which was Mr Gatewood, and told him about Maceo.

'If he suits you,' he said, 'it's all right with me. I don't have to play with him. All I want is music, so you get anybody you like.'

The first night we played Big Maceo rocked the house and I didn't have to sing but one or two songs. So the boss came to me and told me:

'You sure do know a blues singer when you see one.'

And he gave me a bottle of Gatewood Special. Me and Big

Maceo got in my car, we went home and on our way we talked about getting a trio.

We got a boy that we called Little T to play the drums. He could play and sing popular songs, too, and we could play anywhere. So we added one more to the band, we called him Little Joe. He was a bass player and he could really walk a bass. People would stand and look at him play and we got a lot of good jobs playing together in theatres, night clubs and for cocktail parties, and then we added one more to the band. He was Buster Bennett and played saxophone.

In 1945 we made some records together for Columbia, *Partnership Woman*, *Roll Them Bones*, *Bad Luck Man Blues*, *Wandering Man Blues*, and they all turned out good.

Little T got a job with a band, Buster got him a band of his own and Big Maceo got a job to travel on the road, where he was getting more money. So that left me alone.

I got a letter asking me to go to New York, at the Café Society. I went there, stayed for two years and was sent to Texas for two months.

When I came back to Chicago, Big Maceo was playing with Tampa Red at the Flame Club. Tampa wanted to go to Georgia to see his people and got me to play until he got back.

After that I went back to New York where I received a letter from Big Maceo's wife, telling me that he had had a stroke and was paralysed. I went to see him. He got all right, went back to work at the Flame Club and I went back to New York.

Some time later I received another letter telling me that he had had another stroke in a barber shop and that he had to be carried home. So I went to see him again, he couldn't walk at all. I stayed in Chicago to be close to him.

We used to argue and fall out with each other, but no licks were ever passed. He knew more about real music than

I did but I knew more about the real blues and the arguments was because he would tell me to make the right chord.

'It don't sound right to me,' I would answer.

I would hum my song to him and he'd say:

'You's singing all right but the chord you's playing is wrong. It's not chords anyway, it's just sound.'

And he would make the chord on the piano and tell me to sing.

'Don't play, for God's sake!'

I would get mad and we would argue again, but no licks was passed, and we would get a bottle of whisky and take a few drinks, then start back to playing.

'OK, Bill,' he'd say to me, 'we will play your way when you's singing and you play my way when I'm singing, please.'

So that's how we was doing to get along playing together.

'When I am singing,' he told me, 'please make chords, don't just sit there, holding your guitar and making sound. Do what I do. When I make C, F and G and D on a diminished chord you make it, too.'

He would make it on the piano and tell me to find it on the guitar. I would keep on going up and down the neck of my guitar until I'd find the chord that sounded like what he made on the piano.

'That's the boy,' Maceo would say. 'Now you do that when I'm singing.'

And that's how I learned how and what chord I was making when I played the blues. But even today the sound I was making is better when I'm playing. When my song sounds good to me and for me to really sing the old blues that I learned in Mississippi I have to go back to my sound and not the right chords as the musicians have told me to make. They just don't work with the real blues. Just like I used to tell Big Maceo and a lot of other musicians: the blues didn't come out of no book and them real chords did, and I told him and others that the real blues is played and sung the way you feel and no man or woman feels the same way every day, and I say that if he or she did they would go crazy.

Big Maceo was a good friend of mine but we would always argue about playing. I know that he knew more about music than I did but not the blues. He was known all over by *The Married Life Blues*, *Texas Blues* and a lot of other good ones. He played with Tampa Red for a long time, made records with him, played with Big Bill and made twelve records with him. He could play most any kind of music and played with a lot of artists.

As I said before, Big Maceo's family lived in Detroit, Michigan. I've known him since 1941. He told me that his birthday was on March 30 and that he was born in 1905. Every year on March 30 he would give a birthday party and it would take at least fifteen of us musicians to throw him down because he weighed 245 pounds and was six feet tall. But that's the way we all celebrate one another's birthday party by throwing him or her down and hold them. All of us would then give him or her a lick with a strap or a board and some time there would be from twenty-five to thirty of us musicians to give a lick apiece, and before we would hit the lick we would have to call our name so who we hit would know who hitted him when we got around and turned him or her loose or let him get up.

Big Maceo was a favourite of the blues world and he was liked and known by all singers in the USA. He was a member of two Musician Local Unions, in Chicago and in Detroit. I do believe that everybody that likes the blues loved Big Maceo. He lived with his wife and daughter in Chicago, died February 26, 1953, and was shipped to Detroit to be buried there on March 3.

I was with him last September 1952 and we had a ball together, just before I left for London, England. It looks like every time I leave him something happens to him. But we all can say that one of the greatest blues singers is dead and gone in the person of Mr Major Merriweather, better known as 'Big Maceo'.

A man like TAMPA RED has got a style of his own, playing guitar with a bottle neck on his little finger, sliding up and down the guitar strings. He's the first one I've ever seen or heard doing that. But he's not the only one who does it. Some of the others is Elmore James, Muddy Waters, The Night Hawk and Kokomo Arnold.

There was another man going around Chicago saying that he was the real Tampa Red, but we soon caught him and told him he was wrong. I told him he couldn't play as well as the real Tampa Red, because I know the real one and was at his house nearly every day. I don't call what these men are doing stealing but it was really copying after Tampa. This man heard Tampa's records back in the 'twenties, he liked his style, so he learned to play like Tampa and tried to sing like him. But nobody in the world can do that because there is only one Tampa Red and when he's dead, that's all, brother.

Tampa Red has recorded some real good songs, some of which was hits, such as *Tight Like That*, *Hard Travelling*, *My Gal Is Gone*, *When Things Go Wrong*, *Let Me Play With Your Poodle*, *She's Going To Sell My Monkey* and many other good ones. He's been recording for RCA Victor ever since I know him.

I met Tampa Red in the studio in Chicago in 1928. He was then playing a silver-looking guitar and could play it, too. Him and Georgia Tom was playing together, but since then he has used as piano player a man called Forty Five, and also Blind John Davis, Big Maceo, Johnnie Jones and he made some records with the Hokum Boys and some with two guitars: Willie Bee played guitar for him and also a boy called L. C. McKinney. I have never played with him on records, but we have played together on shows and for parties. He's a good-hearted man and a good man to get along with. He's quiet all the time but he can tell some funny jokes, too.

Tampa Red's birthday is on December 25. [b] Every year all the musicians go to his house to eat and drink, talk about different blues and songs, and give him a good beating with a strap. Sometimes it takes from twelve to fifteen men to hold him down and sometimes there is about thirty of us musicians at this birthday party. Some hold him down while the others march around and hit him, not light but hard and he hollered sometimes. That's the way blues singers celebrate, and sometimes there was three of those parties in each month, but maybe in different towns.

Everyone that goes to the party carries a big bottle of whisky. Sometimes, too, the one that was giving the party plays sick to keep from getting a beating.

Me and Tampa Red would go fishing and hunting together. Some time we would catch some fish and some time we would catch nothing. It would cost us about five dollars each to go fishing because we had to buy bait to fish with, gas for my or his car and the important thing was our bottle of whisky or gin, and he liked the best when it came to drinking.

I remember once we went fishing and caught no fish. On our way back Tampa stopped and bought some from a fish market in town and he said to me:

'I'll carry this to my wife. She won't know no difference.'

'I don't know, Tampa, your wife is smart, you know we've tried to fool her about other things and she would find out we was lying.'

'But she can't tell who caught the fish,' he said. 'I will tell her I cleaned them myself.'

So we went in the car and went to his house. When we got in, Tampa said:

'Honey, here's some fish I caught and I cleaned them, too.'

When he said that I got close to the door because any time me and him had done something wrong or when she caught us in a lie she would throw us out. I stayed at the door so I wouldn't have far to go when she got mad, because she was a strong woman. He knew it and I did too, because she had thrown us out before, so he was calling her 'Honey' and 'Darling' and she was batting her eyes right fast and looking at the fish we brought to her.

She pulled her eyeglasses down on her nose, then looked at Tampa Red:

'Both of you is lying. You bought this fish.'

'No, Mrs Tampa,' I said, 'he caught them.'

'Where's the ones you caught, Bill?'

'I didn't catch any.'

'And Tampa caught none either. He bought this. I can tell it by the eyes. This fish has been dead for a month or more and kept on ice. I'm gonna knock the hell out of both of you.'

She was looking for a stick to hit us with and we ran downstairs, got in my car and drove away as fast as we could. We went to buy a bottle, had some drinks and laughed about it.

'I told you so!'

LONNIE JOHNSON had a different style of playing a guitar— we called his style 'thumping a guitar'. He made a lot of good selling records of blues like *Falling Rain Blues, Love Story Blues, In Love Again, Jelly Roll Baker, Tomorrow*, and many other good ones. He has played with a lot of good bands and a lot of good artists like Louis Armstrong. Texas Alexander plays something like Lonnie Johnson.

I remember I came to St Louis, Mo. in 1921 and I met Lonnie and his brother. They called him Buddy Johnson. Then Buddy was playing the piano and Lonnie was playing the violin, guitar, bass, mandolin, banjo and all of the things that you could make music on, and he was good on either one he picked up and he could sing too, just as good.

Lonnie told me he was born in New Orleans in 1894, but he looked to be, in 1952, about forty-seven years old.[c] Anyway I heard a blues recorded by him in Chicago in 1923. He said he learned how to play the hard way. He plays with a pick all the time.

I have never played with Lonnie, but we was together on some shows and on some parties. He's about five feet and ten inches tall. Me and him went to fishing together and it would do me more good to see him catch a fish than it would if I had caught one, because he could holler so loud. He would always say:

'I got him, Bill, he ain't so big, but he's big enough to bite my hook, he's big enough to make the skillet stink.'

And sometimes he caught about twenty-five fishes in one day. He liked to fish very much. We was living in Chicago at that time.

JOE MCCOY had a way of playing a guitar not like his brother or his cousin. He also wrote some real good selling blues and jump tunes. His biggest hits was *Oh Red What You Gonna Do?*, *Why Don't You Do Right?* and a lot more.

Joe's home was in Mississippi, where he was born and raised. I knew his brother Charlie, but he had another brother who was a preacher.

Joe told me he was born in 1900 and he died in 1951. I was at his funeral, and the same day there was a big funeral somewhere else in Chicago. I was at both of them. The other funeral was at a big church and there was more than two thousand people there, even the man who Joe made all his biggest hits for, Mr Mayo Williams.

I left that funeral and went to Joe's. It was in a funeral parlour and there was about twenty people there. Three cars went to the graveyard and my car was one of them three. Mr Williams did not go to Joe's funeral and did not talk about Joe that day.

The other man was an undertaker and had a big funeral parlour on 74th Street in Chicago. Even Memphis Minnie wasn't at Joe's funeral and none of his old friends, such as Johnnie Temple, Herb Morand, Odell Rand, Horace Malcolm and T. C. Williams, the men who played with Joe on all his records and in night clubs.

Joe stopped playing the blues in 1937 and preached for a while. He got married again and had two children by his last wife. I've seen them at his funeral. They was big girls then. His brother Charlie McCoy died the same year.

SONNY BOY WILLIAMSON had a special way of playing the blues on a French harp, better known as a harmonica. He could blow it and sing at the same time. He made some good blues, some of which was hits, like *Cold Chills Blues, Cut That Out, Black Panther Blues, Decoration Day Blues, Elevator Woman, Keep Rubbing On The Old Thing* and a lot more good selling blues. He was a favourite of the blues singers and he made records with a lot of artists and played in clubs with them, such as Lonnie Johnson, Big Bill, Josh Altheimer, Blind John Davis, Bob Call, Walter Davis, Memphis Slim, Sunny Land Slim, Eddie Boyd, Joe Williams and a lot of others.

Sonny Boy was about six feet tall, very dark and with a lot of hair on his head. In 1948 he was playing at a place called the Plantation Club when he got stabbed in the head on his way home. He made it home but died before they could get him to the hospital. The Plantation is in Chicago on 31st Street. He was shipped to Jackson, Tennessee, to be buried. That was his home. He was thirty-two years old when he died. He was stabbed in the head with an icepick— that's a real sharp piece of steel that they use to break up ice with.

He was a good-hearted boy, and free-handed as he could be. He would give you anything he had, he would give the shirt off his back to his friend, and he had a lot of them, too.

Me and Sonny Boy and Memphis Slim played together for a long time and every time Sonny Boy would get drunk he would jump on me or Slim for a fight. Sometimes we would fight him and some other time we would go off and leave him arguing. Then when he would finally find us he would start crying and say to me and Slim: 'Why did you all leave me?' and we would talk nice to him.

He would then buy a bottle of whisky, hand it to one of us, start crying and saying: 'You all sure treat me bad.'

While he would be crying and talking, me and Slim would be drinking. When he'd stop crying and look at the bottle he'd say: 'Who drank all my whisky?'

Then he would want to fight again and some time one of us would have to fight him because he was real strong. But it did never last long.

Sonny Boy was married to a very nice girl that looked after him. I say she was a mother and a wife to him. She helped him writing his songs and helped him to learn how to sing them. She could rhyme a song and had a wonderful handwriting.

I first met Sonny Boy in 1934. He had just come to Chicago from Jackson, Tennessee, not so far from Memphis, Tenn. Jackson was his home, where his family lived at. I saw his mother and brother.

There is a boy in Arkansas, who plays nearly like Sonny

Boy Williamson. There is just a little difference in their names—one is Sonny Boy Williams, he's a light-skin man, and Sonny Boy Williamson is dark skin. ^(d) He's the real old Sonny Boy and he did love to blow his harp and could really blow it.

I loved to play with Sonny Boy and all the blues singers liked him. I remember once that he came to my house.

'Let's go to the ball game,' he said to me.

'I have no money, I told him, and it costs 1.25 to get in and we need something to drink.'

So he said:

'I'll buy the ticket and a bottle of whisky.'

So I said:

'OK, we'll go to see Satchel Paige pitch.'

So we went and we drank all the way to the park. We got there, got a seat and went on drinking. We had to wait about thirty minutes before the game started, we finished our bottle and both of us went to sleep. The man who took care of the park came and woke us up.

Sonny Boy asked the caretaker:

'When does this game start?'

'Next Sunday,' he said, 'this one is over and it's time to go home if you've got one.'

There was fifty-two thousand peoples in the White Sox Park that day. We hadn't seen Satchel Paige or heard nobody say anything, so when me and Sonny Boy got to his house there was a lot of boys and girls there who had seen the game and was talking about it.

Every time that someone would tell about something that had happened Sonny Boy would say:

'Now, sure 'nough, is that true? Well, I be damned!'

'Was you there?' some of them would ask.

'Yes, but I did not see that. When did it happen, in the first game or the last one? It was supposed to be a double header wasn't it, if not I'm going out there and get my money back, won't we, Bill?'

'Yes, Sonny Boy,' I said, and he would ask his friends to tell us about the game.

'Was there really fifty-two thousand peoples there?'

'Yes,' they said, 'and you all shouldn't have went to sleep.'

Then he would just laugh.

PETER CLAYTON was known and has recorded under the name of 'Doctor Clayton'. He made some good selling records, for the RCA Victor Company, with Blind John Davis and Ransom Knowling. He didn't get famous until 1941, when he made *I Am Going To Murder My Baby*, *Doctor Clayton Blues*, *Gin Head Woman Blues*, *Pearl Harbour Blues* and some others.

He told me one day that he was born in Africa and had come to the USA to go to school, in St Louis, Mo. He started going out with a girl, he and her got married and he got a job in a factory.

His wife had four kids and they was doing fine for six years. I saw them over there at that time.

One day he went to work and when he came back home that night his house had burnt down, his wife and all four of his kids was burnt to death in the house.

After that he left St Louis and came to live in Chicago. That was in 1937. He started to drink, gamble, lay around the joints and rough places and he learned to sing the blues. He was a popular and a ballad singer before he lost his family in the fire, and he could really sing.

Doctor Clayton was a good-hearted boy. He wouldn't get a room, he wore tennis shoes in winter time and slept on pool tables and in alleys and basements, anywhere he could, because all the money he made from singing he would drink it up or lose it in some kind of game.

He got sick with pneumonia and died in 1946. There was ten people at his funeral and just three went to the grave-yard to see him buried. That was me and my wife and Tampa Red. He was buried in Chicago, where he died.

I have never heard or seen any of Doctor Clayton's people and never heard him speak of his family, but I don't believe that he had no people in the USA. He had a very good education and was a very intelligent man before he lost his family in St Louis.

GEORGIA WHITE is a good piano player. She plays blues and boogies and she's good at both. She has made some good selling blues and boogie-woogies. Her big blues song was *Trouble in Mind*, but Richard Jones wrote that in 1922.

She told me she was born on March 9, 1903. She is five feet seven inches tall, weighs 185 pounds. She's dark skinned, good-looking, very easy to get along with, good-hearted and real friendly.

I played with her in a night club in Chicago in 1949 and a while in 1950. I never made a record with her, but I have been in the studio when she was recording. She has re-corded for RCA Victor, Columbia, Vocalion, Okeh and Decca.

She was my pianist for a while. I had a band called The Laughing Trio. She would always tell us some kind of funny joke before we started to play.

Alfred Wallace was the drummer and he weighed 260 pounds, he was twenty-three years old and could really beat those drums, and he also could sing the blues, the big city blues.

There was a girl there whose name was Saddie. We called her Black Saddie and she would holler at Alfred and say:

'Why in the hell don't you sing something, and don't laugh so much, we didn't come here to hear you laughing, we came to hear you play and sing!'

That's how we got that name of 'laughing trio'. And we did good together.

Before Georgia White started playing with me, she and a girl trumpet player had an all-girl band, a twelve-piece band, and they broke up. In 1950, after having played with me, she got a real good job in a small town just out of Chicago, and she's still out there now.

CURTIS JONES, he had a way of playing piano—I haven't never heard nobody play like him or even try to play like him.

He made some real good blues songs, some of which was hits, like *Lonesome Bedroom Blues, You Got To Change Your Mind* and a lot of others.

He never did play with nobody because he was difficult to play with. Nobody could learn his style.

He was from the West, out in Tulsa, Oklahoma. He's thirty-seven years old and is married. (e)

He used to play in a lot of the night clubs in Chicago and was always in trouble with the Musicians' Union and had to pay fines. He would be late with his dues or just wouldn't pay his tax.

Curtis was a real good-hearted boy, but so forgetful. . . . I remember once he came to my house and asked me to move him and his wife in my car. He just had a box and one trunk, very small, and one suitcase and a radio.

'OK,' I told him, 'I'll take you if you buy the gas, because I haven't got a licence to charge you.'

'That's what I know,' he answered, 'and that's why I come to you to get moved.'

Where he had to move to was out in Morgan Park, about twenty-five miles from where I lived at.

So we went to his house and loaded up his things and started out. When we got to Morgan Park I asked him:

'What street is the place in?'

'I don't know yet,' he said.

So I stopped the car and he got out and left me and his wife sitting in the car. He stayed away for about two hours and when he came back I said:

'Did you find the place?'

'Yes,' he answered, 'on that street there I see a sign "room for rent".'

We went to this house and they only rented rooms to single men, so he came to the car and told his wife:

'It's a place for me but not for you, so you'll have to go back with Bill until some places get vacant for man and wife.'

So I took his wife home with me and she stayed with me and my wife until there was a vacant room and soon there was.

When MEMPHIS SLIM first came to Chicago and I met him there, he was playing and singing exactly like Roosevelt Sykes. That was in 1939. I told him about playing like Roosevelt, which he denied, but I knew better that he was certainly playing like Roosevelt.

So he made some records, just him playing the piano and another boy playing a tube with a string and a stick on one end of the string and the other end running through the bottom of the tube, he picked that string and pushed that stick back and forth to change the tone. Together they made some blues called *Feeling Low Down, Beer Drinking Woman,* and they was real good ones, too.

Me and Memphis Slim got to be good friends and I liked him very much. As he wasn't working at that time I got him on rehearsing some songs and he recorded with me. We made *Rock Me Baby Blues, Walking Blues, What Is That She Got?, Saturday Evening Blues, Conversation With The Blues.* Since

Big Bill, 1925

William Mitchell, Big
Bill, Memphis Slim,
and Washboard Sam

Top: Teddell Saunders
('Blind Sonny Terry')

Centre: Merline Johnson,
Lester Melrose and
Ransom Knowling

Left: Lonnie Johnson

Lester Melrose and Tampa Red

Big Maceo and Peetie
Wheatstraw

Memphis Minnie

Left to right, standing: Jazz Gillum, Tampa Red and Little Bill Gaither. *Sitting:* Jack Dupree and Big Bill with Tampa Red's dog which 'drank whisky just like we did and helped us sing'.

Big Bill at the Iowa State College
('Mopper's Blues')

Big Maceo

Lil Green

Washboard Sam, 1931

Big Bill, 1953

that time he has made a lot of recordings with me and other artists.

In 1940, February 18, (f) my piano player Joshua Altheimer died, so I asked Memphis Slim to play with me and so he did. We played at the 1410 Club, at the Ruby Tavern, in New York at Town Hall, the Regal Theatre, the 8th Street Theatre, the Beehive in Chicago and many other places.

So one day I finally told to Memphis Slim: 'You's good enough now to go on your own. You don't need Big Bill or no other blues singer with you. Just get you some good musicians to play with you and you'll be Memphis Slim just like I'm Big Bill.'

And so he did. He got a man on alto sax called Atkins, a drummer called Eddie Pain, a bass called Brease, and on tenor sax the boy was Cotton. And Memphis Slim is going big in the USA. He made some hit songs with his band.

His alto sax player was the first I ever heard who could blow two horns at the same time. I didn't believe it when Slim told me he had a man in his band who could do that. I went to hear his band one night and I got close up to Atkins and he put a clarinet and an alto saxophone in his mouth at the same time and it sounded just like two men playing. He's the best I've ever seen and heard.

Now Memphis Slim has a good six-piece band and every man he has is a good musician. The big hit songs he got on record are *Motherless Child Blues* and *Every Day I Have The Blues*, and he has a lot of other good ones out with his band.

Memphis Slim is six feet six inches tall. He's got a wife and four kids. I have seen his father, too. They have the same name: Peter Chatman, and his older boy has the same name, too. His birthday comes on September 3. We would have to outrun him on his birthday because when he would blow out the candles on his cake he would start running out of the house.

I do remember once at his party we all was trying to catch him and the police thought it was a gang fight. When we caught him the police caught us too, and was going to put us all in jail. So I talked to them and told them to come in the house with us so we could show them what was going on. So they did and after that Slim told them to sit down, have some drinks and eat some cake while we gave Slim the works.

There was thirty of us there that day and also Slim's wife, kids and father. Everybody laughed together with the police and after the whipping of Slim we all got a big drink, and started playing music and dancing, girls and boys together.

When I first told Slim that he was playing like Roosevelt Sykes he got mad at me, but he found out what I meant; he changed and went to playing like Memphis Slim. When we used to play together, everywhere we went the people said that we was brothers. Now there is another boy called Eddie Boyd who plays and sings just like him. He sings more like Memphis Slim than Slim did for Roosevelt.

He was called Memphis Slim because he comes from Memphis, Tennessee. He was born and raised around there.

I remember once me and Slim had just come back from New York.

'Let's get drunk,' he said.

I said OK, so we went to the liquor store and bought a fifth of Grand Dad Whisky, a 100 Proof, a fifth of Gordon Gin and a bottle of champagne. When we opened it the champagne all jumped out of the bottle. We had never drunk or seen champagne opened before, we had paid sixteen dollars for it and lost it all.

So we sat down and took a drink of our whisky and chased it with Gordon Gin. When we drunk it all up, oh, boy, were we two drunk men and we had to be taken home one at a time.

When I woke up I was in his bed at his house, and was I sick and hungry!

I played for LIL GREEN for two years as her guitar player. I wrote some songs for her, like *My Mellow Man* and *Country Boy, Give Your Mama One Smile* and some more that I fixed up for her. I wasn't really writing them songs— I just hummed the tune until Henry, the piano player, and the bass player Ransom Knowling, could find the right chords to fit the tune. I hummed to them then she would sing the words that I'd wrote down for her.

Ransom, the bass player, was a good musician, and so was Henry, the piano player. Me, Henry and Ransom was on tour with her all over the South, in every State in the South of the USA.

Of course she got too big for a little group like us, just three pieces, guitar, piano and bass. So she dropped us one at the time. Ransom was dropped after the third tour. I was dropped after the fourth tour and then Henry went to New York with her; he was dropped there and she got a big band.

I went to see Lil at the Apollo Theatre in 1945 and 1946. Both times she was glad to see old Bill and it made me feel good to know that she hadn't forgotten the ones she had started out with. And when she would come to Chicago she would call Big Bill, Ransom and Henry and fix a big dinner for us, but she would eat most of it herself and then tell us to help ourselves.

I did like working for Lil Green because she paid us well and would buy food and plenty whisky for us. She always kept two or three bottles for us, but I've never seen her take a drink or smoke a cigarette. During the time I played with her, some people said she was drinking. But I know better, because me and Henry have put some whisky in a bottle of orange pop one night and gave it to her. She didn't know that there was whisky in the pop and she drank it. And I know she got sick from drinking that pop with the whisky in it.

MEMPHIS MINNIE, who's real name is Minnie McCoy, is a good guitar picker and a good blues singer. She made some good-selling blues. Her first big hit was *Bumble Bee Blues* on which her husband played guitar with her. They played two guitars: she played the lead and her husband, Joe McCoy, played the accompaniment.

That was in 1928 for Vocalion, which is the same company as Columbia. Later on she and her husband parted and she made some recordings with Black Bob, a piano player.

Later again, she got married to Little Son Joe who played guitar, too. They made some good blues together. He played accompaniment and did most of her songs, such as *Me And My Chauffeur, Looking The World Over, Dirty Mother For You, Have You Seen My Man Today?*, and they made together the *Black Rat Blues*, the *Black Rat Swing* and many other good ones.

There was another woman going around Chicago saying she was Memphis Minnie. But when I saw her I said: 'Hell, no, that's not Memphis Minnie, because the real Memphis Minnie can pick a guitar and sing as good as any man I've ever heard. This woman plays like a woman guitar player.'

Memphis Minnie can make a guitar speak words, she can make a guitar cry, moan, talk and whistle the blues. And I know that because I played with her all around. Me and Memphis Minnie played the first contest between blues singers that was ever given in the USA, in 1933, on my birthday, June 26.

The hall was crowded, everything was free and all the musicians that could get in the place was there and every musician had brought a bottle. The prize for me and Minnie was a bottle of whisky and a bottle of gin and we had three judges.

I had to play first. It was on the first floor and they was looking in the windows, both black and white people. We had to play two songs each. Mine was *Just A Dream* and *Make My Getaway* and her two songs was *Me And My Chauffeur* and *Looking The World Over*.

All the musicians played until the time for the contest. It did not start before one-thirty and by that time me and Minnie was really loaded.

Everybody was saying:

'Is that man going to play against that poor little weaker woman? He should be ashamed because any man should beat a woman playing a guitar.'

And one white man walked up to me and said:

'You know you can beat that woman playing and anybody in here knows that you're the best blues player around and anywhere else.'

Of course they had never heard her play or sing because when she would come to Chicago and make records her husband would take her back to Memphis. So this white man comes back to me and says:

'Bill, is this thing going to be done fair?'

'Yes, sir,' I said. 'We have the three best blues singers and players for judges.'

'Who are they?' he asked.

'Sleepy John Estes, Tampa Red and Richard Jones.'

'Well, they know the blues,' he said. 'It's OK then. I just wanted it done fair because all the people are saying they know you can play better than Minnie.'

'I don't know about that,' I said to him, 'but I'm gonna try to win those two bottles so I can get in a corner and drink until I get enough.'

So he laughed and said:

'If you need anything for this party, just call me and I'll send it over.'

There was about forty white people at the party, so at one-thirty Tampa Red called me to the stand and the crowd went wild. I stayed there for ten minutes before I could start my first song.

So I sang *Just A Dream* and they liked it very much. Then I sang *Make My Getaway* and I got down off the stand.

Tampa Red called Memphis Minnie to the stand and everybody got quiet. She first sang *Me And My Chauffeur* and the house rocked for twenty minutes, then she sang *Looking The World Over*.

John Estes and Richard Jones went to the stand, picked Minnie up and carried her around in the hall until her husband saw them, got up and told them: 'Put her down, she can walk.'

He was jealous of any man. So Memphis Minnie won the two bottles and I just waited until they gave them to her. I took the whisky, ran away with it and drunk it. She called me dirty names but I still drank the whisky and said, 'OK, baby.'

I always did like Minnie very much and I've known her for a long time. She told me she was born in 1900, on June 24. She's five feet and five inches tall, she weighs a hundred pounds and has dark skin. She was born in Mississippi and was raised around Memphis. I have seen her brother and sister.

Me and her have played in night clubs all over the States together. I have heard some other women playing guitar but never as good as her. She's still alive in Chicago, a member of Local 208 of the Musician's Union, and still playing the guitar as good as ever and singing the blues. (g)

TOMMY McCLENNAN had a different style of playing a guitar:

you just make the chords E, A or B and just rack your finger across all strings and sing the blues, and change from E to A to B just when you feel like changing. Any time will do. You don't have to be in no hurry. Just close your eyes.

Tommy made some good selling blues, songs like *Bottle Up And Go*, *Gin Head Woman*, *Goodbye Baby* and a lot of others. Some of his songs was never released because he had the wrong words in them.

About *Bottle Up And Go*,[1] when it came out all the Negroes didn't like him no more, just on account of one verse:

The nigger and the white man playing seven up
The nigger beat the white man and was scared to pick it up
He had to bottle up and go.

In Mississippi we didn't mind being called nigger, because we called one another nigger and all the people called us that way. In Chicago and New York, they don't use that word. But that was Tommy's first time in the North. The Northern Negro uses that word, but not when there is white people or light-skin Negroes around. The black Negro doesn't like for a light-skinned Negro to call him or her black. There's been a lot of blood lost on account of them words, just nigger and black. But me and Tommy and a lot more don't mind because we was used to it.

*

Tommy was born in Yazoo City, Mississippi, in 1908. His birthday is in April. He's five feet and seven inches tall and weighs about 130 pounds, and he's real dark skinned.

When Mr Melrose, who is a white man, went to get Tommy I told him what he should do to keep out of trouble in Mississippi, but he told me that he knew and that he was a white man, too.

[1] *Bluebird* 8373.

'It doesn't matter in Mississippi,' I told him. 'You's a Northern white man and they don't like you down there if they see you around Negroes, talking to them. Get some Negro out of town to go and talk to Tommy.'

But no, he wouldn't do like I told him and he did get in trouble—and a lot of it too, because he had to run and leave his car and send back after it and leave money for Tommy to come to Chicago. When I saw him he laughed and said:

'Bill, you was damn right, they don't like me down there.'

Tommy lived on a farm about fifteen miles out of Yazoo City and there ain't but one road, that means one way to go out there and one way to come back and you have to pass the bosses' house both times, so they know a stranger's there and they hate it.

'They don't call me a white man down there,' Mr Melrose told me. 'They call me a Yankee. What does that mean, Bill?'

'I told you they don't like a white man from the North out on their farm or anywhere they have five or six hundred Negroes working. I told you that you might get hurt out on one of them farms or camps.'

'Get hurt, get hurt, hell, they nearly killed me, and they would have done it if I hadn't run like hell. I'll certainly never go down there again.'

So he used to send me all the time after artists. He never did go down South again.

*

When Tommy recorded about eight sides for RCA Victor, I was there with him in the studio and I told him about it that day:

'Tommy, you's gonna get in trouble with that song. Don't sing *the nigger and the white man*, just sing it this way, it means the same thing:

The big man and the little man playing seven up
The little man wins the money and was afraid to pick it up
He had to bottle up and go
But he got mad at me:
'Hell, no, I'll never change my song.'

So he made it his way. I knew he was right, the way he felt about it, because I sang the same words in another song of mine before Tommy was born, but I knew better than to do that in the North, because I had lived there for about three years before I recorded and I knew the Negroes didn't like them words. So I told Tommy about it, but he just said, 'The hell with them.'

That same day, when Tommy was recording, I called some friend on the telephone and he told me to bring Tommy to the party that night, and I did. The house was full of blues singers and the people told me to get Tommy to sing. I went to Tommy, but I told him:

'Don't sing that *Bottle Up And Go*, please.'

'The hell with them, I'll sing my song anywhere I want to.'

So I just stayed close to him because I knew there would be some trouble when he would get to that verse. And there was. I had to put Tommy out the window and me and him ran about five miles to another friend of mine's house where we got a drink.

'I told you that would happen, didn't I?'

'Yes you did, and they made us bottle up and go, but I'm going back and get my guitar.'

'There's no need.'

'Why, Bill?'

'You have some of it around your neck.'

'Just the cord and a piece of the neck. Let's go back there. I'm going to make them pay for my guitar.'

'Yeah, you go back there, but Big Bill is going home,

where you'd better go too, if you want to ever get back to Yazoo City alive.'

So me and him went to my house.

*

The Northern Negroes don't like to be called nigger and black by a light-skinned Negro. They just don't like it at all. But in a place where it's all black and brown-skinned Negroes, they don't care about calling each other nigger and black. But if a white or a light-skinned man or woman comes in, don't say it, please. If you just got to talk and use this kind of words, please don't use them in the North.

The musicians, both white and black, use nicknames. The black musician calls the white musician 'old fay' and the white musician calls the black musician 'old spade', and they never get mad about it at all; they like to be called nicknames.

There is even a few white men who can play the blues, like Frank Melrose, for instance. They always run around with Negroes and play with them. Sometimes we blues singers would call them Negroes too, and they wouldn't mind at all. They would say to us, 'Let's play some Negro music,' and they could play as well as a Negro, but they couldn't sing the blues. They could say the blues words and some of the blues they could sing was of the kind that we call big-city blues and dressed-up blues, but not the real Mississippi blues. They could play and sing the kind of blues that Jelly Roll Morton, Speckled Red, Jimmy Blythe, Blind John Davis, Carl Sharp and a lot of other big-city blues players and singers play.

*

The light-brown-skinned Negro sings:
> *The blacker the berry the sweeter the juice*
> *I want a real black woman for my special use.*

And the real black Negro sings:

Don't want no black woman to bake no bread for me
Because she's black and evil and might poison me.

If a half-white Negro sings either one of the songs he will be beaten up by the black women or men: the black man gets mad because he's singing about his sister, but the black man always marries a light-skin woman and a light-skin man always marries a black woman. Seldom shall you see a black man and a black woman together and I have never heard a black man or woman say, 'I'm proud to be black.' Not me.

WASHBOARD SAM is a good blues singer. He wrote one blues called *The Longest Train I've Ever Seen* and he made a lot of good blues that sold well on records. I wrote many blues for him. He made some of them which was hits, like *Somebody Changed That Lock On My Door, She Never, Somebody's Got To Go, Who Was That Here A While Ago, Mama Don't Allow That, Flat Foot Floogie, Your Time Now, Back To Arkansas, Digging My Potatoes, Stop And Fix It, Outskirts Of Town, Baby Don't You Tear My Clothes* and many others written by me that he recorded and that was good sellers.

He could sing very well and he made his music on a washboard. He used seven thimbles on the end of seven of his fingers and rubbed them down and across the washboard to change his tone and rhythm with his songs.

He had many artists to play with him, like Bob Call, Ransom Knowling, Judge Riley, Memphis Slim, Roosevelt Sykes, Sax Mallett, Blind John Davis, Joshua Altheimer, Buster Bennett. I played on most all of his records because I wrote songs for him and I learned him how to sing the blues with music. He used to sing out of tune, but I showed him how to sing and keep time on his washboard.

Washboard Sam was my half-brother. I believe it because once my mother found out that my father had bought an eighty-acre farm about thirty-five miles from where we was living and my father had another woman living there. That was Washboard's mother.

One morning my mother came in my room and told me to get up. It was about four o'clock.

'Where is we going at this time of the morning?' I asked her.

'We's going hunting for a skunk.' I didn't know she was talking about my father. 'Get the shotgun and hitch up the fastest two horses we got to the new buggy and put food enough to last all day because we might not get back until tomorrow.'

I was glad to get a chance to drive the best horses my father owned because he never allowed me to drive them at all when he was at home. I always had to drive and ride mules. So we got ready and started out.

At about eleven o'clock we was in this little town called Walnut Ridge. My mother got out of the buggy and talked to a white man called Mr Victor Boges. He knew my mother very well because she had cooked for his father. When she got through talking, she came back to the buggy, gave me some ginger bread and told me to drive down that road 'until I say stop', and I did just that.

So I drove for about half an hour, then she said:

'Stop right here and wait until I come back.'

She got out, went to the back of the buggy and got the shotgun.

'Mother, do you see a skunk?'

'Yes, and I smell them, too.'

But I didn't smell nothing. Then she put two shells in the old double-barrel shotgun and went walking up to a house. When she got close enough, she called my father. His name was Frank, and when she yelled 'Frank', I saw the back door open and a woman coming out running as fast as she could, half dressed, and I laughed. My mother saw her too and the old shotgun went off. My father came out a window and went down through a corn field. The old shotgun went off again. Then me and mother started for home.

'Mother,' I asked her, 'you didn't come here for no skunk, did you?'

'Yes, son,' she answered, 'and I found two of them in their den.'

She was really mad at my father because tears was falling down and I got mad at him, too, when I saw her crying. When we got back home that night she went to another white man at about a mile from us. She called him to the door. His name was Mr Margral.

'What do you want, Mittie?' he said.

'I want to talk to you, sir.'

He told her to come in, they met in the porch and talked there for a while.

I could hear some parts of the conversation:

'I want to sell a farm,' she told him.

'What farm? Are you crazy? That's all you and them fifteen children got.'

'Nossir, not that one, the one on Walnut Ridge.'

'Ah, you know about that one, do you? How did you find out?'

'A little bird told me about it.'

He laughed.

'OK, Mittie, just as you say. Meet me in town tomorrow and you'll get the money.' And that's what she did.

About two weeks later I went out to feed the mules and found my daddy sleeping in the barn. He said:

'Go to the house and bring me some bread, I'm hungry.'

I went in the kitchen, got the bread and came out, but my mother stopped me:

'Where is you carrying that bread? To feed a skunk?'

'No, mother, it's for my father . . .', and I started crying. All the other children came running up to me and I told them about father sleeping in the barn, and the fifteen of us started crying. My mother laughed and said:

'Go get that skunk and bring him in the house. I'll make coffee for him.'

So we all went to the barn and got him, but before he would go in the house he said:

'What did your mother call me or just what did she say?'

'She called you a no-good tail-dog,' I said.

'No,' my sister said. 'She called you a long-head mule.'

And all of us got into an argument and my sister, the one who's just like my father and whose name is Gustavee, she yelled at the rest of us:

'Mother said bring the skunk in, I'll make coffee for him.'

Then he told my brother Jim to go in the house get that skunk killer and bring it out.

'I shall not go in the house before I see you with it.'

We all laughed. He meant the old shotgun.

After three or four days he was getting his regular meals again and we all fifteen children was happy.

So that's why I do believe that Washboard Sam is my half-brother because this happened in 1910 and Washboard was born that same year, maybe that same day.

Some years later my father took me and my brothers Jim and Jerry with him and that's when I saw Washboard and his two sisters. His name is Robert and his sisters' names are Rosalee and Mary. When he saw her, my brother told my father:

'That one is just like my sister Mary, and she's got the same name.'

'She is your sister,' my father replied, 'and he's your brother Robert.'

So my father went to see these children and he told

Washboard's mother not to call either one Broonzy, because of that old shotgun, and they went in their grandfather's name, Brown. So today Washboard Sam is Robert Brown.

All of this happened in the State of Arkansas in 1910 and I was seventeen years old then. It is in 1916 that I've first seen Washboard Sam, I was twenty-three, had been married and I was going to see them often. In 1918 I went in the army and I didn't see Washboard no more until 1925 in Memphis. He was a big boy then.

In 1932 he showed up in Chicago. He lived with me for a long time. I started him to sing and play a washboard and got him to make records for RCA Victor. He recorded for them up until 1947.

At that time he got an easy job, but a crazy and dangerous job, too. A policeman; that's what he is now in Chicago. He should make a good policeman and know how to arrest people because he's been arrested so many times, and I always had to go and get him out of jail. He was always into something in them old times. But he's a good boy now, and a good policeman, too. He's married and got two kids and always manages to get home when he gets off from work— his wife told me that. (h)

The following information was supplied by the author prior to publication of this American edition:

Sleepy John Estes
(a) Later reported by Big Bill to have died in Chicago, March 1953, Sleepy John Estes has been found, blind but musically still active, in Brownsville, Tennessee, in 1962, by blues specialist Bob Koester, who recorded him for his Delmar label.
Estes declares that he was born near Ripley, Tennessee, January 25th, 1904.
Part of this Big Bill story may be based on true facts or on hearsay, but of course the dates have been changed.

Tampa Red
(b) Interviewed by Y. B., Tampa Red said he was born in Smithville, Georgia, January 8, 1903. This was confirmed by some official document.

Lonnie Johnson
(c) Several dates have been mentioned for Lonnie Johnson's birth. New Orleans, February 8, 1894 is most likely to be the correct one, as also mentioned on his passport.

Sonny Boy Williamson
(d) There is some confusion here: the singer and harmonica player then living in Arkansas is Rice Miller, now popular under the name of Sonny Boy Williamson (Trumpet and Checker records). Sonny Boy Williams is a singer and pianist who was active in Chicago during the forties.

Curtis Jones
(e) Interviewed in Europe where he lives since January 1962, Curtis Jones declared that he was born in Naples, Texas, August 18, 1906.
Memphis Slim Altheimer

(f) Questioned about this date, Big Bill was absolutely affirmative. Nevertheless, it seems to be certain that Altheimer recorded later that year and died November 18.

Memphis Minnie
(g) Sleepy John Estes, questioned by Bob Koester, said that he didn't remember about this contest. It might be poor memory from one side or the other. These contests were quite common. Maybe Estes forgot about this one, or maybe the judges were not exactly as mentiond.
Since this was written, Minnie's second husband, Little Son Joe (Ernest Lawlers), died, in 1961. She herself has had a bad stroke in 1960 and lives, partly paralysed, in Memphis, Tenn.

Washboard Sam
(h) It seems that it is in this story about Washboard Sam that Big Bill has been the most inspired by imagination or pure fantasy. Their half-brotherhood, though quite possible, is doubtful, having its source more probably in the fact that they were long-time partners in Chicago and that the habit of calling each other "brother" was not rare amongst blues singers. It is, of course, unbelievable that Washboard Sam ever was a policeman, but Big Bill must have imagined this as a good joke, owing to Sam's highly erratic way of life.

150

ENVOI

ALL of these blues players and singers would be real glad to hear something good said or done for them right now and not after they's dead. Why wait until their death? Is it because a dead man or woman can't talk or can't ask for no money?

Well, I guess the men got disgusted with the old idea of cutting records that made millions of dollars and not getting any of it. They had to keep a job to make a living for himself or herself and their family, because they didn't get enough money to live on from the records they made. And some of them was treated like an old mule when he gets too old to pull a plough or a wagon: they either put him in a pasture where he'll starve to death, or they'll shoot him to get rid of him.

As for me, I would love to pick up a book and read a story about Big Bill Broonzy. I wouldn't care if it's just a story about how I live or how drunk I was the last time that they saw Big Bill. I would enjoy reading it because it could be true.

But when you write about me, please don't say I'm a jazz musician. Don't say I'm a musician or a guitar player—just write Big Bill was a well-known blues singer and player and has recorded 260 blues songs from 1925 up till 1952; he was a happy man when he was drunk and playing with women; he was liked by all the blues singers, some would get a little jealous sometimes but Bill would buy a bottle of whisky and they all would start laughing and playing again, Big Bill would get drunk and slip off from the party and go home to sleep.

Some blues singers can and do sing and don't drink, but not Big Bill—he loves his whisky, he's just a whisky-head man.

DISCOGRAPHY

by Albert J. McCarthy

Revised and enlarged by Ken Harrison and Ray Astbury

This discography is a 'name' listing only, of Big Bill Broonzy including pseudonyms, and details recordings that Big Bill made during his entire career which ranged from 1927-57. There are many groups which are believed to have been under Big Bill's leadership, but which, until more information is available, we have thought best to leave out of this work. We wish to record below the assistance given to us by collectors and discographers over the past months.

K. H. , R. A.

ACKNOWLEDGEMENTS

Yannick Bruynoghe (Belgium)
John Godrich
Derek Coller
Hughes Panassie (France)
Wolfie Baum (Germany)
Jack Mitchell (Australia)
Charles Delauney
Brian Knight
Chas. E. Smith
Max E. Vreede

Trevor Huyton
Mike Wyler
Ruth Lokitz (MGM)
Wanda Cyghe (Mercury)
(Blues Appreciation Society)
Don Brown
Dave Carey
John Norris
Bernard Holland

LABEL ABBREVIATIONS

Amadeo-Van	Amadeo-Vanguard (Germany)	OK	Okeh
ARC	American Record Corp.	Or	Oriole
Austr-Mer	Austroton-Mercury (Germany)	Para	Paramount
Ban	Banner	Per	Perfect
Bb	Bluebird	Per	Period (LP)
Ch	Champion	Ph	Phillips (Dutch)
Chess	full name	RBF	Record, Book and Film Club
Co	Columbia		
Cq	Conqueror	Ro	Romeo
Design	full name	Saga	full name (pre-recorded tape)
Fkwy	Folkways		
Fon	Fontana (Dutch)	Stry	Storyville (Dutch)
Gen	Gennett	Sup	Superior
JScy	Jazz Society (French)	Te	Tempo (English)
Lon	London (English)	TR	Top Rank (English)
Mel	Melotone	UnA	United Artists
Mer	Mercury	Van	Vanguard
Mldcs	Melodisc (English)	Verve	full name
Nixa	full name (English)	Vg	Vogue
		Vo	Vocalion
		Vrs	Varsity

COUNTRY ABBREVIATIONS

(Au)	Australia	(F)	French
(D)	Danish	(G)	Germany
(E)	English	(H)	Holland
		(Sw)	Swedish

BIG Bill; vcl,g;acc prob. John Thomas(vcl effects probably g)   c.1927
     House rent stomp   Para rejected
     Big Bill blues   -
     Gonna tear it down (bed slats and all)   -
     Tod pail blues   -
BIG BILL AND THOMPS: vcl,g;acc John Thomas(talking,g)   c. November 1927
20159-2   House rent stomp   Para 12656-A

BIG BILL AND THOMPS: vcl,g; acc John Thomas(g)   c. February 1928
20373-2   Big Bill blues   Para 12656-B

     vcl,g; acc John Thomas(talking,g)   c. October 1928
20922-1   Down in the basement blues   Para 12707-B
20923-2   Starvation blues   -   -A

SAMMY SAMPSON: Big Bill Broonzy(vcl,g); acc Frank brasswell possibly on
on -; definitely on remainder   New York, April 9, 1930
9599-2   I can't be satisfied   Per 157, Or 8025a, Ro 5025A
9600-1   Grandma's farm -   Per 187, Or 8086b, Ro 5086B
9601-2   Skoodle do do   Per 157, Or 8026b, Ro 5026B

BILL WILLIAMS AND SAMMY SAMPSON: Bill Williams(vcl-1,g-2); Big Bill
Broonzy (vcl-3, g-4); Georgia Tom (p)
9621-1   Tadpole blues 1?,2,3?,4   Per 179, Or 8068b, Ro 5168B
9627-1   Bow leg daddy 1?,2?,3,4   Per 163
     note: Per 163 as by "SAMMY SAMPSON"

BIG BILL JOHNSON: Big Bill Broonzy(vcl,g)   Richamond Indiana, May 2, 1930
GE 16569   I can't be satisfied   Gen 7230
GE 16570A   Bow leg blues   Gen rejected
GE 16571A   Tadpole blues   Gen   -
GE 16572B   Grandma's farm   Gen   -
GE 16573   Skoodle do do   Gen 7210, Ch 16015
     note: Frank Brasswell possibly sings and accompanies on
            guitar on above sides.

BILL AND SLIM: Big BillBroonzy(vcl,g); Frank Brasswell (vcl,g)
                               Richmond Indiana, same date
GE 16581   Papa's getting hot   Ch 16015, Vrs 6038
     note: Vrs 6038 as by "MELLOW BOYS" titled "Watch
            out mama"

SAMMY SAMPSON AND HANNAH MAY: Big Bill Broonzy(vcl,g); Hannah May
(vcl); Georgia Tom(p, vcl on -1)   New York, September 15, 1930
10031-2   Pussy cat blues -1
                    Per 173, Or 8058a, Ro 5058A, Ban 32138
10032-2   What do you call that
                    - ,   - ,   - ,   -
10033-1   Court house blues   Per 170B, Or 8034b, Ro 5034B
     note: Masters 10031/2/3 are in ARC files as "Hannah
            May and Bonny Thomas".

WILLIAMS AND SAMPSON: Bill Williams(g); Big Bill Broonzy(g) New York,
                                           September 16, 1940
10036-2   Guitar mess around   ARC rejected
10037-2   Barrelhouse rag(williams, sampson?)
                    Per 172, Or 8042b, Ro5042B

SAMMY SAMPSON: Big Bill Broonzy(vcl,g)   New York, same date
10042-1   Police station blues
                    Per 199, Or 8123a, Ro 5123A, Bam 32301
10043-1   They can't do that   - ,   -b,   - B,
BILL WILLIAMS AND SAMMY SAMPSON: Bill Williams(g); Big Bill Broonzy(g)
                                     New York, same date
10045-2   No good buddy   Per 179, Or 8068a, Ro 5068A

SAMMY SAMPSON: Big Bill Broonzy(vcl,g); Georgia Tom(p)　　New York,
　　　　　　　　　　　　　　　　　　　　　　　　September 17, 1930
10052-1　　　　　State street woman
　　　　　　　　　　　　Per 0201, Or 8125a, Ro 5125A, ban 32393
10053-2　　　　　Meanest kind of blues Per 186, Or 8085, Ro 5085
10054-2　　　　　I got the blues for my baby - ,　　　- ,　　　-

BIG BILL JOHNSON: Big Bill Broonzy(vcl,g) R　　　　Richmond Indiana,
　　　　　　　　　　　　　　　　　　　　　　　November 19, 1930
GN-17281　　　　The banker's blues　　　　　Ch 16327, Sup 2604
GN-17282-B　　　The levee blues　　　　　　　　　Ch rejected
GN-17283　　　　That won't do　　　　　　　　Ch 16172
GN-17284-B　　　How you want it done　　Ch 16172, Sup 2560, Sav 501A
　　　　　　　　note: Sup issues as by "SLIM HUNTER".

BIG BILL BROMSLEY: Big Bill Broonzy(vcl,g) Grafton, Wisc. c. May, 1931
　　　　　　　　　How you want it done　　　　　　Para 13084
　　　　　　　　　Station blues　　　　　　　　　　-

BIG BILL JOHNSON: Big Bill Broonzy(vcl,g) Richmond Indiana February 9, 1932
N18382　　　　　Worried in mind blues　　　　Ch 16396, Sup 2837
N18383　　　　　Too too train blues　　　Ch 16400, 50069, Sup 2808
N18384　　　　　Mistreatin' mamma　　Ch 16396,　- ,　　　-
N18385A　　　　　Big Bill blues　　Ch 16400, Sup 2837, Ch 50060, Riv
　　　　　　　　　　　　　　RLP1039, RLP12-113, Lon(E) AL3535
　　　　　　　　　.note: Sup issues as by "SLIM HUNTER".
　　　　　　　　　　Lon(E) AL3535 titled "Backwoods Blues".

JOHNSON AND SMITH: Big Bill Broonzy(g); Steele Smith(bjo)
　　　　　　　　　　　　　　　　　　Richmond Indiana, same date
N18386A　　　　　Brown skin shuffle　　　Ch 16411, 40074, Sup 2836
N18387A　　　　　Stove pipe stomp　　　　　- ,　- ,　　-

STEELE AND JOHNSON: Steele Smith(lead vcl, bjo); Bill Broonzy(vcl,g)
　　　　　　　　　　　　　　　　　　Richmond Indiana, same date
N18388　　　　　Beedle um bum(dorsey)　　Ch 16385, 50058B, Sup 2798
N18389　　　　　Sellin' that stuff(dorsey)　　- ,　- A,　-
N18390　　　　　You do it　　　　　　　　Ch 16426, Vrs 6038
N18391　　　　　Baby if you can't do better　　　　Ch rejected
　　　　　　　　note: Sup issues as by "THE CHICAGO SHEIKS"
　　　　　　　　　　Varsity issue as by "MELLOW BOYS" titled
　　　　　　　　　　"Do it".
　　　　　　　　　Artist credit is not 100% certain on Champion.

BIG BILL JOHNSON: Big Bill Broonzy(vcl,g)　　Richmond Indiana, same date
N18392　　　　　Mr. Conductor man
　　　　　　　　　　　Ch 16426, 50060, Riv RLP1039, Lon (E) AL3535
N18393　　　　　Alright mamma blues　　　　　Ch rejected

BIG BILL: vcl, g　　　　　　　　　New York City, March 29, 1934
11605-2　　　　　Too too train blues
　　　　　　　　　　　Vo 1745, Per 0220, Mel 12570, Ban 32653
11606-3　　　　　Worryin' you off my mind - Pt. 1 (n.c.)
　　　　　　　　　　　Or 8168, Per 0217, Ban 32559
11607-1　　　　　Worryin' you off my mind - Pt. 2- ,　　- ,　　-
11608　　　　　　Shelby County blues
　　　　　　　　　　　Per 1223, Ro 5197, Mel 12599, Ban 32670
11609　　　　　　Mistreatin' mama blues
　　　　　　　　　　　Per 0284a, Ro 5190, 5347, Mel 13049,
　　　　　　　　　　　　Or 8347, Ban 33085
11610-2　　　　　Bull cow blues (willie broonzy)
　　　　　　　　　　Vo 1745, Per 0220, Mel 12570, Ban 32653, JScy AA514
11611-2　　　　　How you want it done? (willie broonzy)
　　　　　　　　　　　Per 0207, Ro 5138, Ban 32436, JScy AA514

BIG BILL AND HIS JUG BUSTERS: Big Bill bBroonzy(vcl,g); acc poss. Jimmy
Bertrand); 2 jugs on; 1 jug and unknown kazoo on - New York City, March 30, 1932
11617   Long tall mama
               Per 0284b, Ro 5347, Or 8347, Mel 13049, Ban 33085
11624-2   M and O blues -   Per 0207, Ban 32436
               note: Intervening masters by ALABAMA RASCALS

BIG BILL: vcl,g; acc by JUG BAND, comprising probably Roy Palmer(tpt); pno
(possibly Jimmy Blythe); unknown vln; jug.   New York City, March 31, 1932
11632   Rukus juice blues Per 0223, Ro 5197, Mel 12599, Ban 32670

BIG BILL: vcl,g; acc Black Bob(p)   Chicago, March 23, 1934
80388   Friendless blues   Bb 5535
80389   Milk cow blues   Bb 5476
80390   Hungry man blues   Bb 5706
80391   I'll be back home again   Bb 5674
80392   Bull cow blues - Pt. 2   Bb 5476
80393   Serve it to me right   Bb 5674
80394   Starvation blues   Bb 5706
80395   Mississippi River blues   Bb 5535

BIG BILL: vcl,g; acc unknown p; bjo.   Chicago, June 14, 1934
80613   At the break of day   Bb 5571
80614   I want to go home   -

BIG BILL: vcl,g; acc Black Bob(p)   Chicago, October 18, 1934
C704   Hard headed woman
               Per 0309a, Or 8420, Ro 5420, Mel 13281, Ban 33314
C705   Dying day blues   Mel 351031

BIG BILL: vcl,g; acc Black Bob(p)   Chicago, same date
C718   I wanta see my baby   Per 0335a, Ban 33490, Mel 13457
C719   Serve it to me right
               Per 0309b, Or 8420, Ro 5420, Mel 13281, Ban 33314

BIG BILL: vcl,g; acc Black Bob(p)   Chicago, October 19, 1934
C720   Dirty no gooder   Mel 351031
C721   Let her go - she don't know   ARC 5-11-67, Cq 8577
C722   Hobo blues   Per 0335b, Mel 13457, Ban 33490
C723   Prowlin' ground hog
               Per 0313a, Or 8433, Ro 5433, Mel 13311, Ban 33344
C724   Mississippi River blues   ARC rejected

BIG BILL: vcl,g; acc Black Bob(p); unknown vln   Chicago, October 20, 1934
C736   C-C rider
               Per 0313b, Or 8433, Ro 5433, Mel 13311, Ban 33344

BIG BILL: vcl,g; acc Black Bob(p)   Chicago, February 26, 1935
85517   Southern blues (williard broonzy)   Bb 5998, 6964
85518   Good jelly (williard broonzy)   Bb 5998

CHARLIE JACKSON AND BIG BILL: vcl duet with g and bjo. Chicago, March 8, 1935
C912   Good jelly   Unissued
C914   Everybody skuddle   Unissued
               note: Intervening master does not feature Broonzy.
               These sides, along with C913, were remade on
               April 2, 1935. There is a guitar and banjo present,
               but it is not known at time of compilation whether
               it is in fact Big Bill Broonzy.

BIG BILL: vcl,g   Chicago, June 20, 1935
C1020   C and A blues   ARC 5-12-65
C1021   Something good   -

BIG BILL: vcl,g; acc Black Bob(p)   Chicago, July 3, 1935
C1060B   You may need my help someday ARC 6-04-62, Cq 8674
C1061   Rising sun shine on   ARC 5-11-67, Cq 8577

BIG BILL: vcl,g; acc Black Bob(p)   Chicago, July 27, 1935
91423   Mountain blues   Bb 6060
91424   Bad luck blues
91425   I can't make you satisfied   Bb 6111
91426   I'm just a bum   Bb 6111, 6964

BIG BILL: vcl,g; acc Black Bob(p); Bill Settles(bs) Chicago, October 31, 1935
96230   Keep your hands off her (willie broonzy)   Bb 6188
96231   Sun gonna shine in my back door some day
                (willie broonzy)   Bb 6188
96232   Good liquor gonna carry me down   Bb 6230
96233   Down the line blues   -

BIG BILL: vcl,g; acc Black Bob(p); Bill Settles(bs)   Chicago, December 16, 1935
C1182-2   Bricks in my pillow   ARC 6-03-55, Cq 8672

BIG BILL: vcl,g; acc Black Bob(p); unknown bs   Chicago, December 16, 1935
C1189-2   Tell me what you been doing ARC 6-04-62, Cq 8674
C1190-2   Ash hauler   ARC 6-03-55, Cq 8672
C1191   Evil woman blues   ARC rejected

BIG BILL: vcl,g; acc Black Bob(p)   iChicago, February 12, 1936
C1245   These ants keep biting me   ARC 7-01-57, Cq 8766
C1246   Big Bill blues   ARC 6-05-56, Cq 8671
C1247   You know I need lovin' (willie broonzy)
                                                 ARC 6-06-56, Cq 8684
C1248   Match box blues   ARC 6-05-56, Cq 8671
C1249   Low down woman blues (willie broonzy)
                                                 ARC 6-06-56, Cq 8684

BIG BILL: vcl,g; acc Black Bob(p); Bill Settles(bs) Chicago, April 22, 1936
C1358   Bull cow blues No. 3   ARC 6-07-57
C1359   Married life's a pain   ARC 7-03-68, Cq 8777
C1360   Black mare blues   ARC 7-01-57, Cq 8766
C1361   Pneumonia blues   ARC 7-03-68, Cq 8777

BIG BILL: vcl,g; acc Black Bob(p); "Heebie Jeebies"(g, woodblock effects)
                                                 Chicago, May 1, 1936
C1374   Big Bill's milk cow blues No. 3   ARC 6-07-57

BIG BILL: vcl,g; acc Black Bob(p); "Heebie Jeebies" (g, woodblock effects);
Bill Settles(bs)   Chicago, May 27, 1936
C1380   W.P.A. blues   ARC 6-08-55
C1381   I'm a southern man   -

BIG BILL: vcl,g; acc Horace Malcomb(p); George Barnes(g on -1); Charlie McCoy
(mandolin)   Chicago, September 3, 1936
C1455   Lowland blues -1   ARC 6-11-72, Cq 8767
C1456   7-11(Dice please don't fail on me)   ARC 7-03-54
C1457   You know I got a reason -1 ARC 6-11-72, Cq 8767
C1458-2   Oh babe don't do me that way (willie broonzy)
                                                 ARC 7-02-54, Cq 8794

BIG BILL: vcl,g; acc Black Bob(p); Bill Settles(bs) Chicago, September 16, 1936
C1473-1   Detroit special   ARC 6-12-59
C1474-2   Falling rain   -
BIG BILL: vcl,g; acc Black Bob(p)   Chicago, October 28, 1936
C1634-1   Black widow spider   ARC 7-02-54, Cq 8794

BIG BILL: vcl,g; acc Black Bob(p); unknown bs.   Chicago, November 19, 1936
   C1688   Cherry hill   ARC 7-03-54

BIG BILL: vcl,g; acc tpt; Black Bob(p); unknown bs; unknown d.-1
                                          Chicago, January 29, 1937
   C1799   Southern flood blues   ARC 7-04-68, Cq 8776
   C1800   My big money (willie broonzy)
                                   ARC 7-11-67, Vo 03170, Cq 8930
   C1801   My woman mistreats me (tpt out) (willie broonzy)
                                   ARC 7-11-67, Vo 03170
   C1802   Lets reel and rock -1 ARC 7 06-64, Vo 02944, Cq 8912
   C1803   Come up to my house   ARC rejected
                note: Cq issue as by "BIG BILL and HIS ORCHESTRA".

BIG BILL: vcl,g; acc Black Bob(p); Bill Settles(bs); Washboard Sam (woodblocks);
Punch Miller (tpt -1)   Chicago, January 31, 1937
   C1807   Getaway   ARC rejected
   C1808   Terrible flood blues   ARC 7-04-68, Cq 8776
   C1809-2   Little bug -1 (woodblocks out) (willie broonzy)
                                   ARC 7-05-57, Cq 8849
   C1810-2   Horny frog (willie broonzy)   -   ,   -
   C1811   Mean old world   ARC 7-07-54, Cq 8913
   C1812   Barrell house when it rains   -   -
   C1813   You do me any old way -1 Arc7-06-64, Vo 02944, Cq 8912
                note: On C1813, Big Bill refers to the tpt as "Mr
                     Sheiks". C1809 as by "BIG BILL and HIS ORCHES-
                     TRA" on ARC.

BIG BILL: vcl,g; acc Josh Altheimer(p); prob. Alfred Bell(tpt)-1; unknown bs;drs.
                                          Xhicago, June 9, 1937
   C1920   Louise Louise blues ARC 7-08-65, Vo 03075, Cq 8914
   C1921   Let me be your winder
                (broonzy) -1   - ,   - ,   -

BIG BILL: vcl,g; acc Punch Miller (tpt); Leeford Robinson(p); Fred Williams(d)
                                          Chicago, July 8, 1937
   C1959   Hattie blues(willie broonzy)(tpt and g out) ARC rejected
   C1960-2   My old Lizzie   ARC 7-10-57, Vo 03122, Cq 8916
   Cl961   Come home early   ARC rejected
   C1962   Advice blues   ARC rejected

BIG BILL: vcl,g; acc Josh Altheimer(p); prob. Alfred Bell(tpt on -1); unknown d.
   C1961-2   Come home early   ARC 7-10-57, Vo 03122, Cq 8916
                                    Fon(F) 682.099, Fon(H) 682.099
   C1961-4   Come home early -1 ARC 7-10-57, Vo 03122, Cq 8916

BIG BILL: vcl,g;acc Josh Altheimer(p); unknown bs. Chicago, August 19, 1937
   C1988-1   My gal is gone   ARC 7-10-66, Vo 03147, Cq 8915
as above: Chicago, August 31, 1937
   C1988-3   My gal is gone   ARC rejected

BIG BILL: vcl,g; acc Josh Altheimer(p); unknown second g; unknown bs.
                                          Chicago, same date
   C1989-2   Evil hearted me   ARC 7-10-66, Vo 03147, Cq 8915

BIG BILL: vcl,g; acc Blind John Davis(p); unknown d Chicago, October 13, 1937
   C2006-1   I want my hands on it (willie broonzy)
                                   ARC 8-02-57, Vo 03304, Cq 8999
   C2007-2   It's too late now (willie broonzy)
                                   ARC 8-01-58, Vo 03252, Cq 9036
   C2008-2   Made a date with an angel (willie broonzy)
                                   ARC 8-02-57, Vo 03304, Cq 8999
   C2009   Play your hand (willie broonzy) ARC 8-04-56, Vo 03400

BIG BILL: vcl,g; acc Blind John Davis(p); unknown bs. Chicago, October 21, 1937
C1959-3   Hattie blues
C1959-3   Hattie blues (willie broonzy)
                                           ARC 8-01-58, Vo 03252, Cq 9036
C2026   Somebody's got to go (william weldon)
                                           ARC 8-04-56, Vo 03400
C2027   Good boy (willie broonzy) ARC 8-03-54, Vo 03337, Cq 9035
C2028   I want you by my side (willie broonzy)   Vo 04041
C2029   Border blues   ARC 8-03-54, Vo 03337, Cq 9035

BIG BILL: vcl, g; acc Bill Austin(ten); Blind John Davis(p); George Barnes(el-g); Oliver Nelson(jug).   Chicago, March 1, 1938
C2145   Sweetheart land   Vo 04041
C2146   It's a lowdown dirty shame   rejected

BIG BILL: vcl,g; acc Punch Miller(tpt); Josh Altheimer(p); Fred Williams(d); poss. bs on -1;   Chicago, March 30, 1938
C2157-1   Got to get ready tonight   Co 04095
C2158-1   Trucking little woman (broonzy)(no gtr)
                                     Vo 04205, Cq 9074, Co 37783, 30085
C2159   Unemployment stomp (broonzy)   Vo 04378, Cq 9148
C2160-1   Why did you do that to me?(broonzy)(no gtr) -1
                                     Vo 04205, Cq 9074, Co 37783, 30085

BIG BILL:vcl,g; acc Josh Altheimer (p); Ransom Knowling(bs)
                                   Chicago, April 5, 1938
C2163-1   It's your time now(broomzy) Vo 04280, Cq 9078
C2164-1   I'll start cuttin' on you   Vo 04095
C2165   Sad letter blues   rejected
C2166-1   The mill man blues(broonzy)   Vo 04280, Cq 9078

BIG BILL: vcl,g;acc Bill Osborn(ten); Josh Altheimer(p). Chicago, May 5, 1938
C2183-2   I'll do anything for your (broonzy)   Vo 04642
C2184   Sad pencil blues (broonzy)   Vo 04378, Cq 9184

BIG BILL: vcl,g; acc George Barnes(g) replaces Osborn. Chicago, same date
C2185-2   New shake-em on down (broonzy)
                                     Vo 04149, Cq 9073, Co 37782, 30084
C2186-1   Night time is the right time No. 2 (carr)
                                     Vo 04149, Cq 9073, Co 37782, 30084

BIG BILL AND THE MEMPHIS FIVE: Big Bill Brooonzy(vcl,g); acc "Mr. Sheiks"(tpt); Buster Bennett(alto); Blind John Davis(p); unknown second g; unknown bs.   Chicago, September 15, 1938
C2324   Let me dig it(mccoy)   Vo 04591, Co 37785, 30087
C2325-1   W.P.A. rag(broonzy)   Vo 04429, Cq 9164
C2326   Going back to Arkansas   rejected
C2327-1   Rider rider blues (broonzy)   Vo 04429, Cq 9165

BIG BILL: vcl,g; acc Blind John Davis(p); unknown bs. Chicago, same date
C2329-1   Living on Easy Street (broonzy)   Vo 04429, Cq 9164
C2330   Good time tonight (broonzy)   rejected
C2331   Trouble and lying woman (broonzy)
                                     Vo 04591, Co 37785, 30087
C2332   I believe I'll go back home   rejected
                     note: MASTER C2328 does not feature Big Bill.

BIG BILL: vcl,g; acc unknown tpt on -1; ten on -; Josh Altheimer(p); unknown d.
                                   Chicago, September 27, 1938
C2345   Flat foot Susie with her flat yes yes -1 (L. williams)
                                     Co 30135
C2346   Trucking little woman No. 2 (broonzy) Vo 04486, Cq 9165

BIG BILL: vcl,g; acc Josh Altheimer(p); Ransom Knowling(bs)

Chicago, October 24, 1938

C2330-4	Good time tonight	Vo 04532, Cq 9166

as above:

C2381-1	Hell ain't but a mile and a quarter (mcbailey)	Vo 04532, Cq 9166
C2382-4	Don't you lay it on me (big bill)	Vo 04642

"SPIRITUALS TO SWING" LP: Carnegie Hall Concert,NYC, December 24, 1938
Big Bill Broonzy(vcl,g); acc Albert Ammons(p); Walter Page (bs); Jo Jones (d).
Done got wise (broonzy) Van VRS 8524, TR(E) 35/065,
Fon (E) TFL5188, Amadeo-Van AM AVRS8015
note: Above titles are two tracks from Vol.2 of two volume
set. Other tracks by various artists.

BIG BILL: vcl,g; acc Josh Altheimer(p); probably Fred Williams(d).

Chicago, February 6, 1939

C2461	Spreadin' snake blues	rejected
C2462-1	Baby, don't you remember?	Vo 04829, Cq 9284
C2463	Whiskey and good time blues	rejected
C2464	Baby I done got wise	Vo 04706, Vo 30153, Cq 9197
C2465-1	Preachin' the blues	Vo 05096, Cq 9343
C2466-1	Just a dream	Vo 04706, Co 30153, Cq 9197

BIG BILL AND HIS MEMPHIS FIVE: Big Bill Broonzy(vcl,g); probably Buster
Bennett(alto); unknown tpt; Blind John Davis(p); unknown second g; unknown d.

Chicago, February 10, 1939

C2492-1	Fighting little rooster	Vo 05205, Co 37787, 30089, Cq 9342
C2493	Mary blues	Vo 04760, Cq 9278
C2494-1	You can't sell 'em in here	Vo 04829, Cq 9284
C2495	Just got to hold you tight	Vo 04760, Cq 9278

note: Vo 05205 labelled as "BIG BILL".

BIG BILL: vcl,g; acc Odell Rand(clt); Josh Altheimer(p); Ransom Knowling(bs)/

Chicago, May 11, 1939

WC2553	Just wondering	Vo 05043
WC2554	Keep on a-smilin'	Vo 04990
WC2555-1	She never	Vo 04884
WC2556	Woodie woodie	Vo 04938, Cq 9309
WC2557-1	Too many drivers	Vo 05096, Cq 9343
WC2558	You can't win	Vo 04990
WC2559-1	Ride, Alberta, ride	Vo 04884
WC2560	That's all right baby	Vo 05043
WC2561	Please be my so and so	Vo 04938, Cq 9309

BIG BILL: vcl,g; acc Josh Altheimer(P); Fred Williams(d)

Chicago, September 14, 1939

WC2728A	I.C. blues (broonzy)	OK 05601
WC2729A	Cotton choppin' blues	Vo 05149
WC2730	Hot dog mama	rejected
WC2731A	Dreamy eyed baby(broonzy)	Vo 05360
WC2732A	My last goodbye to you (broonzy)	Vo 05259
WC2733A	Don't you want to ride? (broonzy)	Vo 05360
WC2734A	Don't you be no fool (broonzy)	Vo 05404
WC2735A	Just a dream No. 2 (broonzy)	Vo 05259
WC2736A	Tell me what I done (broonzy)	Vo 05149, Cq 9760
WC2737A	Oh yes (pno omitted) (broonzy)	Vo 05205, Cq 9342, Co 37787, 30089

BIG BILL: vcl,g; acc Josh Altheimer(p); Fred Williams(d)

Chicago, December 8, 1939

WC2842A	I'm still your sweetheart baby	Vo 05311

WC2843A	Down and lost in mind (broonzy)
	OK 05641, Cq 9760, J Scy AA562
WC2844A	Let's have a little fun Vo 05311
WC2845A	Messed up in love(broonzy) OK 05641, Cq 9606, JScy AA562
	note: JScy issue gives composer credit to "big bill broonzy".

as above: Chicago, January 26, 1940

WC2897A	Plow hand blues (broonzy) Vo 05452, Cq 9378
WC2898A	Jivin' Mr. Fuller blues (broonzy) Vo 05404
WC2899A	Make my getaway(broonzy) Cq 9794, Vo 05514, Cq 9607
WC2990A	Looking for my baby (broonzy) Vo 05452, Cq 9378, 96)07

BIG BILL: vcl,g; acc Josh Altheimer(p); Fred Williams(d) Chicago, April 17,1940

WC3034A	I've got to dog you (broonzy) Vo 05563, Cq 9606
WC3035A	Last year blues (broonzy) Vo 05514
WC3036A	When I had money (broonzy) Vo 05563, Cq 9605, 9790
WC3037	You got to hit the right lick rejected
WC3038A	What is that she got? (broonzy) OK 05601, Cq 9606
WC3039	Merry go round blues rejected

BIG BILL: vcl,g; acc Josh Aotheimer(p); Washboard Sam(wbd)

Chicago, June 10, 1940

WC3080-A	Medicine man blues OK 05758, Co 37691, 30068, Cq 9762
WC3081-A	
WC3081-A	Looking up at down OK 05698, Cq 9761, Co(F) BF 384
WC3082-A	Midnight steppers OK 05758, Co 37691, 30068, Cq 9762
WC3083-A	Lone wolf blues OK 05698, Cq 9761

BIG BILL: vcl,g; acc Blind John Davis(p); Fred Williams(d)

Chicago, September 20, 1940

WC3305A	Hit the right lick (broonzy) OK05869, Cq 9608
WC3306A	You better cut that out (broonzy) OK 05919, -
WC3307A	I wonder what's wrong with me (broonzy) - Cq 9759
WC3308A	Bed time blues(broonzy) OK 05983, -
WC3309A	Merry go round blues (broonzy) OK 05869, Cq 9609
WC3310A	Serenade blues (broonzy) OK 05983, -

BIG BILL: vcl,g; acc Memphis Slim(p); Ransom Knowling(bs)

Chicago, December 17, 1940

C 3508	Lonesome road blues Ok -6031
C 3509-1	Gettin' older every day(broonzy) Ok o6116,Cq 9794
C 3510-1	That number of mine(No.158)
	OK 06080, Cq 9928, JScy AA 528
C 3511	My gal is gone OK 06031
C 3512-1	I'll never dream again OK 06080
C 3513-1	Rockin' chair blues(Rock me baby blues)
	OK 06116, Cq 9794, 9928, JScy AA 528

note: JScy issues under titles in brackets. Artist credit of JScy issue is "BIG BILL BROONZY" with Memphis Slim(p).

BIG BILL: vcl,g; acc Horace Malcomb(p); Washboard Sam(wbd).

Chicago, May 2, 1941

C 3740-1	Shine on, shine on(broonzy)
	OK 06303, Co 37474, 30041, Cq 9929
C 3741-1	Green grass blues OK 06242, Cq 9929
C 3742-1	My little flower(broonzy) OK 06386
C 3743-1	Sweet honey bee(broonzy) -
C 3744-1	When I been drinking(broonzy)
	OK 06303, Co 37474, 30041, Cq 9931
C 3745	Key to the highway -1 OK 06242,Cq 9932,RBF RF 1

note: -1 Jazz Gillum(hca)added. Unknown bs replaces Artist credit on RF 1 to "BIG BILL BROONZY".

161

BIG BILL: vcl,g; acc Memphis Slim(p); Washboard Sam(wbd).

Chicago, July 17, 1941

C 3903-1	Double trouble(broonzy)	OK 06427,Co 37242,30012,Cq 9930
C 3904-1	Going back to my plow (broonzy)	OK 06484
C 3905-1	I'm having so much trouble(broonzy)	OK 06484,Cq 9931
C 3906-1	Wee wee hours (broonzy)	OK 06552
C 3907-1	Conversation with the blues(broonzy)	OK 06552,Cq 9932
C 3908-1	All by myself(melka)-1	OK 06427,Co 37242,30012,Cq 9930

note: -1 unknown bs replaces wbd.

BIG BILL:vcl,g; acc Horace Malcomb(p); Washboard Sam(wbd).

Chicago, December 2, 1941

C 4082-1	Keep your hand on your heart	OK 06601
C 4083-1	KWhy should I spend my money(broonzy)	
		OK 06630, Co 37461, 30028
C 4084-1	What's wrong with me(melka)	
		OK 6705, Co 37459, 30026, "V"D 260B
C 4085-1	I feel so good(broonzy)	
		OK 6688, Co 37088, 30007, "V"D 496X
C 4086-1	In the army now	OK 06601
C 4087-1	Bad acting woman(broonzy)	OK 6724,Co 37456,30023
C 4088-1	Night watchman blues(broonzy)	
		OK 6705, Co 37459, 30026, "V"D 260B, Co(F) BF 384
C 4089-1	She's gone with the wind (broonzy)	
		OK 06630, Co 37461, 30028

"BLUES IN THE MISSISSIPPI NIGHT" LP: c. 1942
"Leroy" alias Memphis Slim(vcl,p,talking); "Natchez" alias Big Bill Broonzy (vcl,g,talking); "Sib" alias Sonny Boy Williamson(vcl,hca,talking). Big Bill Broonzy talks all the way through this LP; he sings only one stanza unaccompanied and his guitar is heard briefly on "Have you ever been to Nashville" sung by Memphis Slim.   UnA 4027, Nixa NJL 8

BIG BILL AND HIS CHICAGO FIVE: Big Bill Broonzy (vcl,g); Punch Miller(tpt); Buster Bennett(alto); Memphis Slim(p); Judge Riley(d).

Chicago, March 6, 1942

C 4197-1	I'm gonna move to the outskirts of town(weldon)	
		OK 6651, Co 37196, 30010
C 4198-1	Tell me baby(broonzy)	
		OK 6688, Co 37088, 30007, "V"D 496B
C 4199-1	Hard hearted woman(broonzy)	
		Ok 6651, Co 37196, 30010
C 4200-1	I'm woke up now(broonzy)	OK 6724, Co 37456, 30023

BIG BILL:vcl,g; acc Buster Bennett(alto); Big Maceo(p); Tyrell Dixon(bs)/

Chicago, February 19, 1945

C 4380	Doing the best I can	unissued
C 4381	Partnership woman	Co 30143
C 4382	Where the blues began	unissued
C 4383-1	Humble blues	Co 36879, 30002
C 4384-1	Oh baby(broonzy)	OK 6739, Co 37454, 30021
C 4385	Cell No. 13 blues (broonzy)	Co 37164, 30009
C 4386	Believe me what I say	unissued
C 4387	1944 blues	unissued

BIG BILL:vcl,g; acc Big Maceo(p); Tyrell Dixon(d). Chicago, February 24, 1945

C 4414-1	When I get to thinkin'(h.h.melka)	
		OK 6739, Co 37454, 30021
C 4415-1	Roll them bones	Co 36879, 30002
C 4416	Letter to Tojo	unissued
C 4417-1	You got the best go	Co 37164, 30009

BIG BILL: vcl,g; acc Memphis Slim(p); Ransom Knowling(bs); Tyrell Dixon(d).

Chicago, January 28, 1947

CCO 4711-1	San Antonio blues(broonzy)	Co 38070, 30109

CCO 4712-1	Saturday evening blues (broonzy)	Co 37314, 30016
CCO 4713	Martha blues	unissued
CCO 4714	Texas tornado blues	unissued
	note: Co 37314 as "BIG BILL AND HIS RHYTHM BAND."	

BIG BILL: vcl,g; acc Oett Mallard(alto); Bill Casimir(ten); Bob Call(p); unknown bs; Judge Riley(d).

Chicago, September 29, 1947

CCO 4848	Big Bill's boogie(broonzy)	Co 37965, 30101
CCO 4849-1	Just rocking(broonzy)	Co 38070, 30109
CCO 4850	Shoo blues (broonzy)	Co 37965, 30101

BIG BILL: vcl,g; acc Johnny Morton(tpt); Oett Mallard(alto); Bill Casimir(ten); (Bob Call(p); Ransom Knowling(bs); Judge Riley(d).

Chicago, December 19, 1947

CCO 4950	Stop lying woman	Co 30143
CCO 4951-1	Rambling Bill	Co 38180, 30118
CCO 4952-1	Summertime blues	- , -
CCO 4953	Bad luck man(broonzy)	Co 30135

BIG BILL BROONZY AND HIS FAT FOUR: Big Bill Broonzy(vcl,g); Antonio Cosey(alto); Carl Sharp(p); Ransom Knowling(bs); Alfred Wallace(d).

Chicago, January, 1949

2176-1	I love my whiskey	Mer 8122
2177-1	You've been mistreatin' me	Mer 8160
2178-1	I stay blue all the time	-
2179-1	Water coast blues -1	Mer 8122
	note: -1; alto out on this track	

BIG BILL BROONZY: vcl,g; acc Alfred Wallace(d)   Chicago, April, 1949

2497-2	Five feet seven	Mer 8126
2498-2	I wonder	-
2499-1	Keep your hands off her (broonzy)	Mer 8139
2500-1	Mindin' my own business (broonzy)	-

BIG BILL BROONZY': vcl,g.   Paris, September 20, 1951

note: It is known that more than one take was made of many of the tracks on this and the two subsequent Vogue sessions. Where different takes are known, this is indicated by the symbols -1,-2. The symbol -u indicates that it is known that more than one take was made but it is not known which is used on the issues thus indicated.

51-V-4095	House rent stomp(broonzy) -1	Vg(F) 121, LDM 30.037
		Vg(E) V,2076, LAE 12009
		Vg(G) LDM 30.037
51-V-4096	In the evening(leroy carr)	Vg(F) 138,LD 030, LDM 30.037
		Vg(E) V.2073
		Vg(G) LDM 30.037
51-V-4097	The moppin' blues	Vg(F) 142,LD 030, LD 524.30
		Vg(E) V.2076
51-V-4098	Hey,hey baby (broonzy)	Vg(F) 148,LDM 30.037
		Vg(E) V.2075,LAE 12009
		Vg(G) LDM 30.037
51-V-4099	Willie Mae Blues(broonzy)	Vg(F) 148,LDM 30.037
		Vg(E) LAE 12009
		Vg(G) LDM 30.037
51-V-4100	Black, brown and white(broonzy)	Vg(F) 134,LDM 30.037
		Vg(E) V.2077,LAE 12009
		Vg(G) LDM 30.037
-2		Vg(E) LAE 12009
-u		Vg(F) 125,LD 030, LDM 30.037,LD 605.30
	(Per SPL 1114)	Vg(G) LDM 30.037

51-V-4102-1	Low land blues(big bill broonzy) -3, -4	Vg(F) LD 030,LDM 30.037
-2		Vg(G) LDM 30.037
-u		Vg(F) LD 524.30
		Vg(F) 138
		Vg(E) V.2073
		Per SPL 1114
51-V-4103-1	Feelin' low down -5	Vg(F) 142,LDM 30.037
		Vg(G) LDM 30.037
-2		Vg(F) LD 524.30
-u		Vg(E) V.2077
51-V-4104	What I used to do	Vg(F) 125,LDM 30.037
		Vg(E) V.2078
51-V-4105	Make my getaway(broonzy)	Vg(F) 118,LD 030, LDM 30.037
		Vg(E) V.2078,LAE 12009
		Vg(G) LDM 30.037
	Hollerin' and cryin' the blues (broonzy)	Vg(F) LD 030,LD 605.30
		Vg(E) LAE 12009 -6
		Per SPL 1114

notes:-1 Guitar solo
    -2 This track is labelled as "Big Bill Blues" on Vg(F) LDM 30.037 and on Vg(E) LAE 12009, where the composer credit is to "broonzy".
    -3 The label of Vg(E) V.2073 gives the recording date as September 21.
    -4 Labelled as "Feelin' low down" on Vg(F) and (G) LDM 30.037
    -5 Labelled as "Low land blues" on Vg(F) and (G) LDM 30.037
    -6 Titled "Hollerin' and cryin' blues" on sleeve of Vg(E) LAE 12009.

BIG BILL BROONZY: vcl,g.		Paris, September 21, 1951
51-V-4106	Blues in 1890(big bill broonzy)	Vg(F) 131,LD 030, LDM 30.037
		Vg(E) V.2074
		Vg(G) LDM 30.037
51-V-4107	Big Bill blues(broonzy) -1	Vg(F) 134,LD 524.30
		Vg(E) V.2075
51-V-4108-1	Lonesome road blues(broonzy)	Vg(F) EPL 7138, LDM 30.037
		Vg(G) EPL 7138, LDM 30.037
-2		Vg(F) LD 524.30
-u		Vg(E) V.2068,EPV 1107
51-V-4109	When did you leave heaven? (bullock-whiting)	Vg(F) EPL 7138, LD 524.30
		Vg(E) V.2351,EPV 1107
		Vg(G) EPL 7138
51-V-4110-1	John Henry(traditional)	Vg(E) V.2074
-2		Vg(E) LAE 12009
-u		Vg(F) 118,LDM 30.037, LD 524.30
		Vg(G) LDM 30.037

note:-1 this track is titled as "Low down blues" on Vg(F) LD 524.30 and the composer credit is to "williams".

CHICAGO BILL: Bill Broonzy(vcl,g).		London, September 24, 1951
D 467	Keep your hands off	Mldsc 1191, EPM 7-65
D 468	Stump blues	- , -
D 469	Five foot seven	Mldsc 1203, -
D 470	Plough hand blues	- -

note: Artist credit on the EP is to "BIG BILL BOONZY"; there are no composer credits.

BIG BILL BROONZY: vcl,g.   Paris, c. October, 1951
    Make me a pallet   J Scy unissued
    Take me back   -
    Frankie and Johnnie   -
    Hard headed woman   -
    St. James Infirmary   -
    Dying day blues   -
    Friendless funerals blues   -
    Crowded graveyard   -

note: The titles listed above were listed in the Jazz Society catalogue for July/August 1952, as to be issued on LP 6, but this actually appeared as a King Oliver item. It seems doubtful whether these titles were ever issued. A great many titles were taped for this company but details are lacking. It should be noted however, that, in conversation with Hughes Panassie, Big Bill denied ever recording the above titles.

BIG BILL BROONZY "The Blues" vcl,g; acc Ransom Knowling(bs)
Chicago, November 8, 1951

4521-1	Hey, hey (broonzy)	Mer 8271, 71352, MG 36137 Mer(E) MMB 12003, ZEP 10065 Austr-Mer 126031 MCE
4522	Stump blues(broonzy)	Mer MG 36137, MG 20822 Mer(E) MMB 12003 Mer(Sw) kEPI-6563
4523	Get Back (broonzy)	Mer MG 36137, MG 20822 Mer(E) MMB 12003, ZEP 10065 Mer(Sw) EPI-6563
4524-1	Willie Mae(broonzy)	Mer 8261, MG 36137, MG 20822 Mer(E) MMB 12003 Austr-Mer 126031 MCE
4525-2	Walkin' the lonesome road (broonzy) -1	Mer 8271, MG 36137 Mer(E) MMB 12003, ZEP 10065 Mer(Sw) EPI-6563 Austr-Mer 126031 MCE
4526	Mopper's blues(broonzy)	Mer 8284, MG 36137 Mer(E) MMB 12003, ZEP 10065 Austr-Mer 126031 MCE
4527	Iknow she will (broonzy)	Mer 8284, MG 36137 Mer(E) MMB 12003, ZEP 10093 Mer(Sw) EPI-6563

note:-1 On Austr-Mer this title is listed as "Walkin' down a lonesome road".

BOB CALL or Memphis Slim(p) added.   Chicago, same date
note: The sleeve of Mer(E) MMB 12003 lists Bob Call as the pianist on this and the following sessions, but Memphis Slim has claimed to have played the piano on these sessions.

4528-1	Hollerin' blues(broonzy)	Mer 8261, MG 36137 Mer(E) MMB 12003, ZEP 10093

BIG BILL BROONZY(vcl,g); Oett Mallard(alto); Bill Casimir(ten); Ransom Knowling(bs); Judge Riley(d); Bob Call or Memphis Slim(p).

		Chicago, November 9, 1951
4529	Leavin' day (broonzy)	Mer 70039, MG 36137 Mer(E) MMB 12003, ZEP 10093 Mer(G) RJ 41250
4530	Southbound train (broonzy)	Mer 70039, MG 36317, MG 20822 Mer(E) MMB 12003, ZEP 10093 Mer(G) RJ 41250
4531	Tomorrow (broonzy)	Mer 71352, MG 36137, MG 20822 Mer(E) MMB 12003 Mer(G) RJ 41250
4532	You changed(broonzy)	Mer MG 36137 Mer(E) MMB 12003 Mer(G) RJ 41250

BIG BILL AT PLEYELL HALL: Big Bill Broonzy(vcl,g); Blind John Davis(p).
Mezz Mezzrow Concert, Salle Pleyell,   Paris, February 5, 1952

Guitar shuffle -1	Vg(F) LD 605.30
How long blues	-
Nobody knows the trouble -1	-
Feelin' low down	-
It's your time now	-

note: -1 Omit piano.

BIG BILL BROONZY:vcl,g; acc probably Ernest 'Big' Crawford(bs).

		Chicago, February 10, 1952
4649	John Henry	Mer MG 26034, MG 36052, MG 20822, Mer EPI-6058 Mer(F) MEP 14105
4650	Crawdad	Mer MG 26034,MG 36052 Mer EPI-6058 Mer(F) MEP 14105
4651	Bill Bailey(cannon arr: durante-barnett)	Mer MG 26034, MG36052 MG 20822, Mer EPI-6058 Mer(E) YEP 9508 Mer(F) MEP 14105
4652	Make my getaway	Mer 26034, MG 36052 EPI-6508 Mer(F) MEP 14105
4653	Blue tail fly(arr: Burl Ives)	Mer MG 26034, MG 36052, MG 20822, Mer EPI-6059 Mer(E) YEP 9508 Mer(F) MEP 14106
4654	Back water blues(smith)	Mer MG 26034, MG 36052, EPI-6059 Mer(E) YEP 9508 Mer(F) MEP 14106
4655	In the evening(melrose)	Mer MG 26034, MG 36052, MG 20822, Mer EPI-6059 Mer(E) YEP 9508 Mer(F) MEP 14106
4656	Trouble in mind	Mer MG 26034, MG 36052, EPI-6059 Mer(F) MEP 14106

notes: Composer credits listed are from Mer(E) YEP
9508. MG 26034 is a 10" LP: MG 36052 is a
12" LP with reverse by Josh White. There are
no composer credits on MG 26034 label or sleeve

except last three titles listed according to com-
poser(i.e. Bessie Smith, Leroy Carr, Richard
Jones) and not under actual title. This also
applies to "In the evening" on MG 20822

BIG BILL BROONZY: vcl,g.		Paris, March 19, 1952
	Coal black curly hair	Vg(F) EPL 7138,
	(traditional)	LD 524.30
		Vg(E) EPV 1107
		Vg(G) EPL 7138
-1	Hey! Bud blues(broonzy)	Vg(F) Ld 072, LD 605.30
-2		Vg(F) LD 524.30
-u		Vg(F) ELP 7948
		Vg(E) EPV 1o24
		Per SPL 1114
	Do right blues(unknown)	Vg(F) LD 072, LD 524.30
		Vg(E) LAE 12009
-1	Baby, please don't go(broonzy)	Vg(F) LD 072, LD 605.30
-2		Vg(F) LD 524.30
-u		Vg(F) ELP 7948
		CFD 9
		Vg(E) EPV 1024
		Per SPL 1114
		Design 113
		Gala GLP 357
	Letter to my baby(unknown)-2	Vg(F) LD 072,ELP 7948'
		LD 524.30
		Pop SPO 17002
		Vg(E) LAE 12009
		Per SPL 1114
	Kind hearted blues(broonzy)	Vg(F) LD 072, LD 524.30
		Vg(E) EPV 1024
-1	Louise, Louise blues	Vg(F) LD 072, LD 605.30
-2		Vg(F) LD 524.30
-u		Vg(F) ELP 7948
		Vg(E) LAE 12009
	Down by the riverside	Vg(F) LD 072,
	(traditional)	LD 524.30
		Vg(E) EPV 1024
	Stand your test in judgement	Vg(F) 20072, LD 072,
	(traditional)	LD 524.30
		Vg(E) LAE 12009
	Guitar shuffle (broonzy) -3	Vg(F) EPL 7138,
		LDM 30.037
		Vg(E) V.2351, EPV 1107
		Vg(G) EPL 7138,
		LDM 30.037

notes: -1 Labelled as "Coal black curley".
 -2 Composer credit on Pop is to "broonzy".
 -3 Guitar solo

BIG BILL BROONZY AND WASHBOARD SAM: Big Bill Broonzy(vcl,g); Washboard Sam(wbd); possibly Ernest 'Big' Crawford or Willie Dixon(bs).

		Chicago, c. 1952-53
U 7508	Little City woman(broonzy)	Chess 1546, LP 1468
U 7509	Lonesome (broonzy)	- , -
	Jacqueline (broonzy)	Chess LP 1468
	Romance without finance (broonzy)	-

Big Bill Broonzy(vcl,g); Washboard Sam(vcl,wbd); Memphis Slim(p).

	By myself (broonzy)	Chess LP 1468

Washboard Sm (vcl,wbd); Big Bill Broonzy(g); Memphis Slim(p).

	Shirt tail(r.brown)	Chess LP 1468

unknown bs replaces Memphis Slim:

U 7512	Bright eyes(r. brown)	Chess 1545, LP 1468
U 7513	Diggin' my potatoes(r.brown)	- , -
	Never, never(r.brown)	Chess LP 1468

Memphis Slim(p) added:

Mindin' my own business(r.brown)	Chess LP 1468
Horseshoe over my door(r.brown)	-
I'm a lonely man(r.brown)	-

"A TRIBUTE TO BIG BILL" Big Bill Broonzy(vcl,g); Leslie Hutchinson(tpt); Bruce Turner (alto); Kenny Graham(ten); Benny Green(bar); Dill Jones(p); Jack Fallon(bs); Phil Seamen(d)   London, October 26, 1955

It feels so good (broonzy)	Nixa NJ 2016,NJE 1005, NJL 16
Southbound train	- ,NJE 1015, NJL 16
Trouble in mind	Nixa rejected
Whiskey head man	Nixa rejected

note: Kenny Graham listed under pseudonym of "Fred Hartz".

Big Bill Broonzy(vcl,g).   Recorded at a party, later same day

Southern saga (broonzy)	Nixa NJE 1047,NJL 16
When the sun goes down(1.carr)	- , - , Pye PEP 605
Going down the road feeling bad (broonzy)	Nixa NJE 1047, NJL 16, Pye PEP 605

note: Pye EP and Nixa EP and LP sleeve give the title of "When the Sun goes down" as "In the evening".

Rev. Pye PEP 605 - Josh White.

Big Bill Broonzy(vcl,g.   London, October 27, 1955

Saturday evening(broonzy)	Nixa NJE 1005,NJL 16
Glory of love(hill)	- , - Metronome(D) MEP 1093
St. Louis blues(handy) -1	Nixa NJE 1005,NJL 16 Metronome(D) MEP 1093
Mindin' my own business (broonzy)	Nixa NJ 2012, NJE 1015, NJL 16
When do I get to be called a man (broonzy) -2	Nixa NJ 2012, NJE 1015, NJL 16 Metronome(D) MEP 1093
Partnership woman(broonzy)	Nixa NJE 1015,NJL 16 Metronome(D) MEP 1093

Note: -1 Guitar solo
      -2 Nixa EP gives title as "When will I get to be called a man".

Big Bill Broonzy(vcl,g).   Paris, February 10, 1956

Somebody's got to go(broonzy)	Co(F) FPO 080,ESDF 1162 Co(G) C 40286 Co(E) SEG 7674 Co(Au) SEGO-7674
Water coast (broonzy)	Co(F) FPO 080,ESDF 1121 Co(E) SEG 7790
Big Bill's guitar blues (broonzy)-1	Co(F) FPO 080,ESDF 1121 Co(E) SEG 7790
Take this ole hammer(broonzy)	Co(F) FPO 080,ESDF 1121 Co(E) SEG 7790
Rock me baby (broonzy)	Co(F) FPO 080 Co(G) C 40286

Careless love (handy)	Co(E) SEG 7674
	Co(Au) SEGO-7674
	Co(F) FPO 080,ESDF 1162
	Co(G) C 40286
	Co(E) SEG 7674
Diggin' my potatoes	Co(Au) SEGO-7674
	Co(F) FPO 080
	Co(G) C 40286

note: -1 Instrumental.

Big Bill Broonzy(vcl,g).   Baarn, Holland, February 17, 1956

Bossie woman (broonzy)	Ph B08102L
	Ph(E) BBL 7113
	Co WL-111
Texas tornado (broonzy)	Ph BO8102L
	Ph(E) BBL 7113,BBL 7536
	Co WL-111
Trouble in mind (r. jones)	Ph BO8102L,B681555L*
	Ph(E) BBL 7113
	Co WL-111
Martha (broonzy)	Ph B08102L
	Ph(E) BBL 7113
	Co WL-111
Key to the highway (broonzy)	Ph B08102L
	Ph(E) BBL 7113
	Co WL-111
Goodbye baby blues (broonzy)	Ph B08102L
	Ph(E) BBL 7113
	Co WL-111
Tell me what kind of man Jesus is (traditional)	PHh B08102L,430.714BE
	Ph(E) BBL 7113
	Co WL-111
See see rider (traditional)	Ph B08102L,430.714BE
	Ph(E) BBL 7113
	Co WL-111
When I've been drinkin'(broonzy)	Ph BO8102L,430.71BE
	Ph(E) BBL 7113
	Co WL-111
Swing low, sweet chariot(trad.)	Ph BO8102L,430.71BE
	Ph(E) BBL 7113
	Co WL-111

note: "American Folk Blues" sampler LP.
"Wonderful World of Jazz" LP.

Big Bill Broonzy(vcl,g)   Club Montmatre, Copenhagen, May 4, 1956

DGF 33	I'm goin' down the road(trad.)	Stry SEP 316,SLP 114
		Te(E) TAP 23,EXA 61
		Saga STG 8069
DGF 34	Ananias(Tell me what kind of man Jesus is)	Stry unissued
DGF 35	In the evening	Stry SLP 154
DGF 36	This train (traditional)	Stry SEP 316, SLP 114
		Te(E) TAP 23,EXA 61
		Saga STG 8069
DGF 37	I love you so much	Stry SLP 143
DGF 38	Diggin' my potatoes(trad.)	Stry SEP 383
DGF 39	Willie Mae (broonzy)	- ,SLP 154
DGF 40	Bill Bailey won't you please come home (cannon)	Stry SEP 316,SLP 114
		Te(E) TAP 23, EKA 61
		Saga STG 8069
DGF 41	Take this hammer(broonzy)	Stry unissued
DGF 42	John Henry (trad.)	Stry SEP 383
DGF 43	Glory of love (hill)	Stry unissued

DGF 44	The crawdad song(trad.)	Stry SLP 114
		Te(E) TAP 23
		Saga STG 8069
DGF 45	The blue tail fly (traditional)	Stry SLP 114
		Te(E) TAP 23
		Saga STG 8069
DGF 46	Black, brown and white(broonzy)	Stry A 45053,SLP 114
		Te(E) TAP 23
		Saga STG 8069
DGF 46A	Guitar blues (broonzy)	Stry SLP 114
		Te(E) TAP 23
		Saga kSTG 8069
DGF 47	Hey, Bub blues(trad. arr; broonzy)	Stry SLP 114
		Te(E) TAP 23
		Saga STG 8069
DGF 48	Goodnight Irene(leadbetter, lomax)	Stry SPL 114
		Te(E) TAP 23
		Saga STG 8069
DGF 49	Sixteen tone(trad.)	Stry SEP 383
DGF 50	Pennies from heaven	Stry unissued
DGF 51	In a shanty in old shanty town (little, siras, young)	Stry SEP 316,SLP 114
		Te(E) TAP 23,EXA 61
		Saga STG 8069

Big Bill Broonzy(vcl,g).   Copenhagen, May 5-6, 1956

Swanee River	Stry SLP 154
Swing low sweet chariot	-
Big Bill talks	Stry unissued
Take this hammer	Stry SLP 143
When things go wrong	Stry SLP 154
Barrelhouse shuffle(guitar rag)	-
Down by the riverside	-
See see rider	Stry SLP 143
John Henry	Stry SLP 154
Diggin' my potatoes	Stry SLP 143
Bill Bailey	Stry unissued
Just a dream	Stry SLP 154
Careless love	Stry SLP 143
Ananias(Tell me what kind of man Jesus is)	Stry SLP 154
Midnight special (trad.)	Stry A 45054,SLP 143
Keep your hands off her	Stry SLP 143
I got a girl	-
You better mind	-
Hey bud	Stry unissued
John Henry	Stry unissued
Glory of love	Stry SLP 143
I get the blues when it rains	Stry SLP 154
My name is William Lee Conley B.	Stry SLP 143
Big Bill talks	Stry SLP 154
Louisiana blues	-

"FOLK SONGS AND BLUES WITH BIG BILL BROONZY AND PETE SEEGER"
Big Bill Broonzy(vcl,g).   Chicago, 1956

Alberta	Fkwy FP 86,FS 3864		
I wonder why	-	,	-
Makin' my get a-way	-	,	-
In the evening when the sun goes down	-	,	-
Love you baby	-	,	-
Crawdad hole	-	,	-
John Henry	-	,	-

Big Bill Broonzy(vcl,g); Pete Seeger(vcl,bjo).   Chicago, same date
>You got to walk that lonesome
>valley   Fkwy FP 86, FS 3864
>You got to stand in judgement   -   , -
>The midnight special   -   , -
>note: These titles were recorded from radio programme
>No.4 on Studs Terkel's Weekly Almanac on Station
>WFMT. Other titles on this LP by Pete Seeger solo.

"BIG BILL BROONZY SINGS COUNTRY BLUES"
Big Bill Broonzy(vcl,g).   New York, unknown date
>Trouble in mind   Fkwy FA 2326
>In the evening   -
>When things go wrong(
>(It hurts me too)   -
>Diggin' my potatoes   -
>I wonder when I'll be called a man! -
>Louise, Louise   -
>Frankie and Johnny   -
>Southbound train   -
>Joe Turner No. 2   -
>Hey, hey baby   -
>Saturday evening blues   -
>note: This session should probably be located after
>the session of November 14, 1956 because of
>the numbering of the two versions of "Joe Turner".

"Big Bill Broonzy - Story"
Big Bill Broonzy(vcl,g) and talking with Studs Terkel.
>   Chicago, November 14, 1956
>Plough-hand blues   Fkwy FG 3586
>C.C. rider   -
>Bill Bailey   -
>Willie Mae blues   -
>This train   -
>Mule ridin'-talkin' blues   -
>Keys to the highway   -
>Black, brown and white   -
>Joe Turner No. 1   -

"Big Bill Broonzy sings Folk Songs"
Big Bill Broonzy(vcl,g).   Chicago, probably November 14, 1956
>Backwater blues   Fkwy FA 2328
>I don't want no woman
>(to try to be my boss)   -
>Martha   -
>Tell me who   -
>Bill Bailey   -
>Tell me what kind of man Jesus is -
>Glory of love   -

"Big Bill broonzy, Sonny Terry and Brownie McGhee"
Big Bill Broonzy(vcl,g); Sonny Terry(vcl,hca); Brownie McGhee(vcl,g); interviewed by Studs Terkel.   Chicago, 1957
>Keys of the highway   Fkwy FS 3817
>Red river blues   -
>Crow Jane blues   -
>Willie May   -
>Daisy   -
>Louise   -
>Shuffle rag   -
>The blues   -
>Beautiful city   -
>Tell God how you treat me   -
>Hush hush   -
>When the saints go marching in -

"Big Bill Broonzy - Last Session"
Big Bill Broonzy(vcl,g); talking with Studs Terkel. Chicago, July   1957

Vol	Title			
	Key to the highway (broonzy-segar)	Verve V3000-5-1,	HMV CLP 1544	
	Mindin' my own business (arr. broonzy)	-	,	-
Vol One	Saturday evening blues(broonzy)	-	,	-
	Southbound train (broonzy)			
	Tell me what kind of man Jesus is (Ananias) (arr. broonzy)	-	,	-
	Swing low, sweet chariot (arr. broonzy)	-	,	-
	Joe Turner blues-1 (arr. broonzy)	Verve V3000-5-2,		-
Vol Two	Plowhand blues(broonzy)	-	,	-
	Going down the road feelin' bad -2 (broonzy)	-	,	-
	Makin' my getaway(broonzy)	-	,	-
	Stump blues -3(broonzy)	-	,	-
	See see rider(rainey)	-	,	-
Vol Three	I'm gonna move to the out- skirts of town(weldon-razaf)	Verve V3000-5-3,	HMV CLP 1544	
	This train(arr.broonzy)	-		,HMV CLP 1551
	Hush hush(arr.broonzy)	-	,	-
	Backwater blues -4 (bessie smith)	-	,	-
	Slow blues -5(broonzy)	-	,	-
	It hurts me too(whittaker	-	,	-
	Kansas City blues(arr.broonzy)	-	,	-
	(In the evening) when the sun goes down -6 (carr)	-	,	-
Vol Four	Worried life blues (merriweather)	Verve V3000-5-4,		-
	Trouble in mind(jones)	-	,	-
	Take this hammer (arr. broonzy)	-	,	-
	The glory of love(hill)	-	,	-
	Louise blues(temple-williams)	-	,	-
	Willie Mae blues(broonzy)	-		,HMV CLP 1562
Vol Five	Alberta(arr.broonzy)	Verve V3000-5-5,		-
	Old folks at home (Swamee River)(arr.broonzy)	-	,	-
	Crawdad song(arr.broonzy)	-	,	-
	John Henry(arr. broonzy)	-	,	-
	Just a dream(On my mind) (arr. broonzy)-7	-	,	-
	Frankie and Johnny(arr.broonzy)	-	,	-
	Bill Bailey won't you please come home (arr.broonzy)	-	,	-
	Hollerin' the blues -8(broonzy)	-	,	-

notes: The HMV issue gives this track two titles, viz. "Joe Turner blues" and "Bogie woogie". The title "Boogie woogie" is in fact the second half of "Joe Turner blues".
-2 titled "I ain't gonna be treated thisaway" on HMV.
-3 titled "Hollerin' blues" on HMV.
-4 titled "The flood" on HMV.
-5 titled "Blues" on HMV. There is no vocal on this track.
-6 titled "When the sun goes down" on HMV.
-7 titled "Just a dream" on HMV.
-8 titled "Slow blues"(Lookin' for that woman)on HMV.
Many more tracks were recorded at this session, some including Brownie McGhee and Sonny Terry. The HMV issues have the talking between Big Bill and Terkel edited out.

DISCOGRAPHY

Since the revised discography was supplied to the publishers, one other LP has been issued which is appropriate to this book. This is "Seeger and Broonzy In Concert," released in England by Transatlantic Records, Ltd., Label XTRA 1006. This LP was produced from previously unreleased material in the possession of Folkways Records, USA. Songs by Big Bill Broonzy in the album include Back Water Blues, This Train, Bill Bailey, and Alberta. In addition, various unreleased tapes are still in the possession of Moses Asch of Folkways Records.

INDEX